EPIC ATHLETES
LIONEL MESSI

Dan Wetzel
Illustrations by Jay Reed

Henry Holt and Company
New York

For Cameron Williams

Henry Holt and Company, *Publishers since 1866*
Henry Holt® is a registered trademark of Macmillan Publishing Group, LLC
120 Broadway, New York, NY 10271 • mackids.com

Library of Congress Cataloging-in-Publication Data
Names: Wetzel, Dan, author.
Title: Epic athletes: Lionel Messi / Dan Wetzel ; [illustrations by Jay Reed].
Description: First Edition. | New York : Henry Holt and Company, [2019] |
Series: Epic athletes | Audience: Ages: 8–12.
Identifiers: LCCN 2019017742| ISBN 9781250295811 (hardcover) |
ISBN 9781250295897 (ebook)
Subjects: LCSH: Messi, Lionel, 1987——Juvenile literature. |
Soccer players—Argentina—Biography—Juvenile literature. |
Futbol Club Barcelona—History—Juvenile literature. |
Soccer—Spain—Barcelona—History—20th century—Juvenile literature. |
Soccer—Argentina—History—20th century—Juvenile literature.
Classification: LCC GV942.7.M398 W48 2019 | DDC 796.334092 [B]—dc23
LC record available at https://lccn.loc.gov/2019017742

Our books may be purchased in bulk for promotional, educational, or business use.
Please contact your local bookseller or the Macmillan Corporate
and Premium Sales Department at (800) 221-7945 ext. 5442 or
by email at MacmillanSpecialMarkets@macmillan.com.

First edition, 2019 / Designed by Elynn Cohen

Printed in the United States of America
by LSC Communications, Harrisonburg, Virginia
1   3   5   7   9   10   8   6   4   2

Also by Dan Wetzel

Epic Athletes
STEPHEN CURRY

Epic Athletes
ALEX MORGAN

Epic Athletes
TOM BRADY

Epic Athletes
SERENA WILLIAMS

Epic Athletes
LEBRON JAMES

1

Greatness

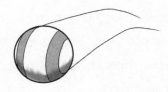

WITH HIS TALENTED RIGHT FOOT, Lionel Messi collected the pass. He was standing on the FC Barcelona side of midfield, maybe sixty yards from the net he was determined to score upon.

No one else inside Camp Nou, the famed stadium of the Barcelona Football Club in Spain, shared Lionel's belief that a goal was possible at that moment. Not any of the tens of thousands of cheering fans. Not any of Barcelona's coaches. Certainly, none of Barcelona's opponents, the players on the Getafe Football Club. And not even his teammates could have fathomed it, even though they'd been taught while practicing against Lionel to expect the unexpected.

How could they think a goal was possible? How could anyone? Lionel was by the right sideline in the middle of the field, with two defenders closing quickly on him and another four or five, plus a goalkeeper, waiting between him and the net.

The expected play, the simple play, even the "proper" soccer play, was for Lionel to find an open teammate nearby, then make a short, crisp, accurate pass in an effort to control possession and slowly build an attack.

That isn't how Lionel Messi played soccer, though. That isn't what brought him here to Spain, on the other side of the Atlantic from his birthplace of Argentina. That isn't what made him a budding international star at just nineteen years old, one of the youngest top division players in all of Europe. That isn't what got him into the starting lineup for Barcelona, or Barça, as its many fans call it, one of the biggest, richest, and winningest clubs in all the world.

From the time he was a small child, pushed by his maternal grandmother, Celia, to play with the older kids in the streets of his native Rosario, Argentina, Lionel had learned to dribble through crowds of outstretched legs and charging defenders.

It wasn't just his footwork that impressed spectators, although that had always been mesmerizing. Onlookers used to say it appeared as if the ball was stitched to his foot, or at least attached on a string, when he dribbled. The description made sense considering as a kid he'd entertain crowds on a street corner by juggling a ball hundreds of times in a row, tapping it into the air over and over without it ever hitting the ground. He was so good at it, he'd leave a hat out to collect donations. Stunned adults would drop coins or bills into it out of appreciation, with Lionel earning valuable money for his working-class family.

But it was more than physical talent that drove Lionel Messi. It was the way he could, in a flash, think of what to do and where to go to escape a defense and push the ball toward a goal. It was mental. It was creative. It was pure soccer. It seemed impossible.

Especially for a guy who'd been considered undersized his whole life, and told as a young kid that he was too short and too small to be much of a player.

At least that is what they said until he whipped by or around or through a defense and scored again. Lionel, as all opponents would learn, even bigger and older ones, was virtually unstoppable. He was this quick, relentless pest, they all agreed.

"La Pulga," they named him in Argentina.

The Flea.

Lionel had come to Spain at just thirteen years old. In spite of his size, his talent was so intriguing that Barça was willing to spend considerable resources to move him and his family to another continent so he'd play for their youth teams. It's common for European football clubs to recruit players like Lionel at a young age, signing them to their junior team.

As part of Lionel's arrangement with Barça, the team paid for the medicine he needed—medicine his parents couldn't afford—to help him overcome a growth hormone disorder. Without the treatments, Lionel's doctors in Argentina believed he wouldn't reach five feet tall, a height that would make a professional soccer career unlikely.

Now, in 2007, facing off against Getafe, he stood five foot seven, still on the shorter side, and presumably not too much of a problem for his defenders.

Little did they realize he'd figured out how to turn his height into an advantage. He was quick, with a low center of gravity that allowed him to shift his weight on a dime. While bigger players still tried to muscle him and knock him down, he could often slip out of the way and leave them foolishly grasping at air. He was like a ghost, disappearing into space, usually with the ball.

Those two charging Getafe defenders were about to learn that lesson the hard way, in front of a packed stadium, a television audience, and the now forever replays on YouTube.

He trapped the pass with his right foot and then with his left, lightly flipped the ball into the air and over the probing leg of the first defender. It wasn't a traditional touch. The ball actually rotated in the air and then, due to all the spin Lionel put on it, magically landed in almost the same spot where it started. That was exactly where Lionel wanted it. As skill moves go, it seemed to defy physics and thus left the defender baffled.

Without hesitation, Lionel slid himself sideways to avoid a collision and then tapped the ball forward and took two steps toward the midfield line. By that point, the other nearby defender was coming in fast, so Lionel flicked it left, not forward . . . and pushed the ball *between the legs* of the unsuspecting defender. In soccer, it's called a nutmeg. It rarely works at the professional level, where everyone is talented and well trained. It was perfectly executed here.

Now Lionel had some open grass in front of him. He dug in and began sprinting down the pitch, still in full control of the ball. The two defenders gave chase, one even had a good angle on him, but Lionel was much too fast to be caught, even though he still had to dribble, which normally slows a player down. The Camp Nou crowd began to murmur and then cheer in anticipation of what was possibly to come. The television announcer's voice picked up a measure of excitement after the nutmeg.

"Oh, brilliant skill from Lionel Messi," he said.

Within an instant, Lionel had left the two defenders in the dust, and as he approached the Getafe goal box, two more came up to converge on him and stop the play. Despite traveling forward at full speed, Lionel was able to tap the ball left, past one defender, shift his body left to avoid contact, then tap the ball back right to avoid the next defender while managing to cut forward and charging, with the ball, into the goal box. He'd somehow, someway split through them. Now each of the first four defenders were harmlessly behind him.

But with one more threat avoided, another emerged. Suddenly, the Getafe goalkeeper was barreling toward him, focused on knocking the ball away and slowing the elusive Lionel Messi down. Lionel had other ideas. Inches before crashing into the keeper, he put the ball on his left foot and shimmied his hips as if he were going to move left toward the front of the goal. As the goalkeeper moved that way, Lionel deftly cut back to the right. The goalkeeper flopped on the ground, helpless to stop Lionel.

The crowd was going wild! It was equal parts shock and delight. At this point, Lionel was still just an up-and-coming player with Barça, not the global icon he would become. He had been one of the youngest to ever make the senior team and the youngest at the time to score a goal for Barça.

He was capable of these kinds of amazing runs, but hadn't yet developed the consistency in scoring that would make him the most productive and dangerous player in the world. Still, he had been considered the future of the club prior to that day. But in that moment, it seemed like the future had finally arrived and become the present.

These flashes of greatness drew comparisons to another soccer star from Argentina, a man named Diego Maradona. Like Lionel, Maradona was short (just five foot five), but had been considered a genius in his day, dribbling the ball and darting through defenders. Maradona, now retired, was hailed, along with the Brazilian Pelé, among the greatest players ever. He had even played for a few seasons with Barcelona and led Argentina to the 1986 FIFA World Cup, where he scored a famous goal that was eerily similar to what Lionel was producing now.

In that match, Maradona had run about sixty-eight yards through six English defenders to score a goal so spectacular it was deemed the "Goal of the 20th Century." Now here was Lionel, who, like all young Argentine players, had grown up watching and worshipping Diego Maradona, reenacting almost the same play. Lionel had traveled about sixty-five yards, and after getting around the goalie, was being approached in desperation by a sixth Getafe defender.

"Brilliant from Messi," the announcer said.

Lionel was running out of room at that point, though. The end line was fast approaching and Lionel was still moving swiftly. His angle on the net was poor and growing worse with each heartbeat. That final defender smartly slid to block what he believed would either be a low shot or a cross to the front of the net. If the defender was successful, then all of Lionel's efforts would go for naught.

Even as a child, though, Lionel had shown an ability to remain calm in the tightest of moments. It could be the final seconds of a tie game. It could be the half second available to decide how to score before losing the opportunity. In his first year with one of his youth teams, he scored one hundred goals . . . in just thirty games. You don't do that by panicking.

And so, with no time to spare and little room to make a play, Lionel Messi knew he needed to thread the needle to score. So, he got under the ball just enough to chip it over the defender, but still managed to hit it hard enough so it would fly into the far side of the net.

Goal. Goal! *Goooooaaaaallllll!*

"Oh, what a goal that is," the announcer shouted. "Have you seen a better goal than that?"

As Lionel ran to the corner to rejoice, his teammates raced toward him in awe, jumping on him in celebration, amazed by what he'd just done. The Getafe players just stood there, stunned, wondering what they possibly could have done to stop that goal. Truthfully, there was probably nothing. Whatever else they might've tried, Lionel likely would have figured out a countermove. Meanwhile, the Barça fans screamed and waved towels and shook one another, like they were trying to wake up from a dream.

"It was the most beautiful goal I have ever seen," said Deco, one of Lionel's teammates.

Pretty much everyone agreed, even those who compared it to that famous one Maradona had scored way back in 1986.

"I hope Maradona can forgive me," said one Barça coach, "but I think Messi's goal is even better."

It was.

But more than that, it was a major step for Lionel Messi on the road to becoming one of the greatest to ever play the sport.

2
Early Life

LIONEL ANDRÉS MESSI was born June 24, 1987, in Rosario, Argentina. His parents, Jorge and Celia, already had two older sons, Rodrigo and Matías. The family would later add a daughter, María. Lionel's father worked as a supervisor at a local steel plant. His mother had been employed at a coil and magnet factory before quitting to raise the kids.

Argentina is a Spanish-speaking country located in the southern part of South America. It sits along the South Atlantic Ocean. Parts of the country are so far south that ships depart there for Antarctica.

The Messi family lived in the Las Heras neighborhood of Rosario, which sits along the Paraná River in the northern part of the country. It counts about 1.2 million residents. Its climate is warm and humid.

The Messis lived in a two-story, concrete home at 448 Lavalleja Street, with a tall metal security fence running along the sidewalk. They were neither poor nor rich by Rosario's standards, although few in the city had any great wealth.

Like almost everywhere in Rosario, the homes were packed tightly together. There was almost no room for backyards or parks. For fun, kids had to play in a lightly trafficked street or maybe a small abandoned lot. Just about any strip of dirt was used. And most often, that meant playing soccer.

Many of the greatest soccer players of all time were raised in busy South American cities just like Rosario. Pelé, Neymar, and Ronaldinho all came from Brazil. Luis Suárez is from Uruguay. And then there was Maradona, the Argentine legend, who grew up in Lanús, about a three-hour drive from Rosario and just outside Argentina's capital city of Buenos Aires.

It is said that due to the crowded conditions of street play and the fact that neighborhood games

could feature twenty or thirty kids, the
were forced to develop superior foot ski
ativity. With so few fields to play on, and ...
existed mostly being dirt, there was no other way to
win than to adapt. You couldn't just outrun someone. You needed to dribble around them, trick them,
fake them out. And even then, another kid would
be there waiting to try to steal the ball. Once these
players moved to actual regulation pitches, as soccer
fields are known, they thrived in the extra room and
on the plush grass where the ball rolled true.

Soccer surrounded Lionel from birth. Both his
brothers played. So too did Lionel's cousins who
lived close by. His father, Jorge, was a very good
player himself, but quit as he became an adult to
join the military and provide for his family.

Then there was everyone else in the neighborhood, who were either playing soccer or watching
soccer. A chief obsession was the Argentina national
team, of course. Lionel was born just one year after
its historic 1986 World Cup victory. Maradona was a
hero; his image was painted in murals that adorned
the sides of buildings all over the country. Lionel
dreamed of being beloved like that and winning a
victory for his country on soccer's biggest stage.

At the age of four, Lionel was given a present: his own soccer ball. He became obsessed with it, constantly dribbling and juggling it around his home. Soon he wanted to join the kids and his older brothers in the street, playing soccer. At the time, he was very young, though, and both short and slight for his age. As a child, he would suffer a broken arm, wrist, and leg because he was so tiny. He was nervous to play, but his maternal grandmother, Celia, encouraged him to get out and try. He quickly got over his nerves. Despite being so tiny, he instantly showed skill, dribbling around older kids and slipping passes and shots through more experienced players.

As he got older, Lionel wanted to do little else other than play soccer. He played in the neighborhood. He played inside his house. When he would walk to the store to run an errand, he would bring his ball and dribble it.

"From then on it was the only present I ever wanted, Christmas, birthday or whatever: a ball," Lionel told Goal.com years later.

When Lionel was four years old, his older brothers played for a small local youth club named Grandoli. Rodrigo was seven years older and Matías five years older than Lionel. Grandoli wasn't a particularly good team. It played and practiced on a beaten-up, mostly dirt pitch. It was not too far from the Messis' home, though. Both of his brothers were promising players, but the team still struggled and was often disorganized. It was youth soccer, something closer to the American Youth Soccer Organization (AYSO), or rec soccer, in America, than to a more competitive environment like a travel team.

One day, Lionel tagged along to his brother's practice with his mother and grandmother. Grandoli had teams in different age groups, and while Lionel's brothers trained on one pitch, a game was about to begin on a different field featuring kids who were six and seven years old. That Grandoli team was down a player, and the coach, Salvador Aparicio, was trying to figure out what to do. That's when he spied Lionel.

He was juggling his ball, bouncing it off his feet or knees over and over without it hitting the ground. Then he was kicking it hard against a wall. Lionel clearly had some skill, Coach Aparicio thought. But he was so little. He was four but looked closer to three. There were going to be players much bigger and more experienced in the game. Could this tiny kid keep up with older, larger opponents?

"I looked up to the stands and saw him playing with a ball," Coach Aparicio told Goal.com. "But he was so small, so we decided to wait for the other player to turn up. But he didn't, so I asked Lionel's mother if I could borrow him."

Coach Aparicio felt any player, even one so young, was better than no player. Lionel's mother was against it. Leo, as she called him, was too little and frail, she said. There was no way he could compete with the older kids. If he played, he would almost certainly get injured. Besides, juggling a ball is one thing, but Lionel had no experience playing in an actual game.

That's when Grandma Celia stepped in. She always believed her grandson was a special person and a special talent. She encouraged Lionel's mother to let the boy play. Coach Aparicio said he'd keep Lionel near the sideline in an effort to prevent him from being harmed. If he started crying, he'd take him off. Lionel wasn't sure, but Grandma Celia practically pushed him out on the pitch. Soon enough, the game was on.

Lionel didn't know what to do. The other boys were taller, stronger, and faster. The ball, onlookers recall, came up to his knees.

"The first time the ball came to him he just looked at it and let it pass," Coach Aparicio said. "He didn't even move."

Lionel decided to overcome his fears.

"The next time the ball came to him, it virtually hit him on the left leg," Coach Aparicio said. "Then, he controlled it and started running across the pitch. He dribbled past everyone crossing his path."

Lionel wasn't just good enough to play, he was good, period. Really good. After that impromptu try-out, Lionel was a member of the Grandoli Football Club. His teammates were all at least a year older than him, but Lionel didn't care. He received some of his first real training, albeit at less than ideal facilities.

"There's a pitch without much grass, filled with dirt and even some rocks," Lionel said.

Lionel was a natural. He could maneuver right around defenders, using skill moves and instincts that players normally don't display until they are much older. He could dribble with either foot, change directions and speed, and had an unusual ability to keep the ball very close to his foot while still moving fast. Even at four and five years old, he wasn't just kicking the ball down the field and then chasing it. He was in control.

"Later, in the youth teams, he scored six or seven goals in every match," Coach Aparicio told Goal.com. "Instead of waiting for the goalkeeper to kick the ball, he would take the ball off him and start dribbling all over the pitch. He was supernatural."

Word began to spread about this talent, the youngest Messi boy. Usually the only people who care about youth soccer, even in Argentina, are the families of the players. That changed when Lionel Messi was playing. People started coming out to watch him play when he was just five years old.

"Immediately he started attracting local attention," Grandoli FC president David Trevez told the BBC. "He was so different from the rest. He would get the ball, go past four or five players and score. For a kid that age, it's very rare to be able to do that.

"People were saying Grandoli had the next Maradona, and when he was playing, people who weren't even connected to the club would come," Trevez continued. "The whole neighborhood would watch the game."

For Lionel, it was just fun. He was a child playing a game, unaware of the fuss he was causing.

"I loved going there because we spent all the

weekends playing with my brothers, my cousins and the whole family," Lionel said years later.

While he played other sports, soccer was his passion. Lionel later looked back and realized that being able to play with so little pressure when he was very young is how he developed a love of the game.

"I don't like to give advice but if I have to say something, I would tell you, enjoy what football is," Lionel said years later about youth soccer. "Learn how to win and learn how to lose, but above all, enjoy."

Soccer would become serious business soon enough.

3

Newell's Old Boys

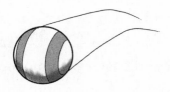

THE ARGENTINE FOOTBALL ASSOCIATION (AFA) is the main professional soccer league in the country. Since Argentina's professional teams aren't as wealthy as those in Europe, many of the country's biggest stars go to play in the British Premier League or La Liga in Spain. The quality of soccer in the AFA is still very strong, though.

Rosario is home to two teams—Rosario Central and a club called Newell's Old Boys. The rivalry between them is intense and divides the city like nothing else. Flag-waving, chant-singing supporters pack each team's stadium, and when not at games, they debate about whose team reigns supreme. Families will even paint the telephone poles in front of their houses to show their support—red and black for Newell's Old Boys or blue and yellow for Central.

You are either for one or you are for the other. The Messis followed Newell's because their father followed Newell's. It was a family tradition.

Newell's Old Boys got its unusual name because it was founded in 1903 by Isaac Newell, an English player and coach who moved to Argentina. It was originally a school where you could get an education as well as soccer training. The term "Old Boys" referenced the boys who had graduated from the school, sort of like "alumni" of a high school or college. The team's nickname is "the Lepers" because back in the 1920s, it played a fund-raiser for a leprosy clinic that treated patients with that disease.

Newell's wasn't just a professional club. It also sponsored youth teams via its soccer academy. These would be the equivalent of high-level travel clubs in the United States. Players in the academy receive training and coaching and then play in tournaments across Argentina.

It also serves as a minor league. If a player signs with Newell's when he is ten years old, then he is obligated to remain with the club throughout his soccer career, unless Newell's renounces the contract or trades the player away. Finding great young talent is the lifeblood of the main team, so both Newell's and Rosario Central often battled to find the best young players. That's why it didn't take long for word of a young dribbling and scoring phenom named Lionel Messi to reach a Newell's scout.

He immediately came to watch Lionel play for Grandoli. At first glance of little Leo, he thought the hype about the kid must have been overblown. Lionel was so small, there could be no way that he was a dominant player, let alone one that he heard the club *must* sign. His nickname at the time was "El Enano" or "the Midget."

Then the game began and Lionel did his thing, cutting around defenders, making crisp passes, and causing opponents to look confused. It appeared he could make the ball do anything he wanted. He had a way of flying around the pitch with the ball, looking like a yo-yo was attached to his foot. In the first half, Lionel scored three goals. No matter how short he was, there was no denying his talent. The scout was sure of one thing: Lionel Messi was going to play for Newell's Old Boys.

That was fine with Lionel. It had been his dream. His family were fans of the pro team, and his dad had even played for Newell's when he was a kid. Additionally, both his older brothers, good but not great players, had recently begun playing for Newell's teams in their age groups.

Lionel could also live at home and get to the soccer academy easily. For some of his teammates, the sacrifice was greater. They came not just from all parts of Rosario but also surrounding towns. Some drove two hours each way for practices and games. For others, the distance was so great that entire families had to move to Rosario. That's how important they viewed the opportunity to play for Newell's.

The Lepers played an offensive style with great passion, creativity, and flair. At that age, they competed in a 7v7 league—seven boys on each side, one goalie and six regular field players, on a smaller pitch. In Lionel's first game, Newell's won 6–0. He scored four goals.

With Lionel as the star, the team became nearly invincible. Despite playing the best competition possible in Argentina, the Lepers went undefeated for three consecutive years—when Lionel was eight, nine, and ten.

Since Lionel and his teammates were born in 1987, they were given a nickname: "The Machine of '87." It was a machine that churned out victories. Contests were often blowouts—10–zip, 15–zip, even 20–zip. Lionel scored one hundred goals in his first thirty games alone and it's believed he pumped in over five hundred goals during his time with Newell's.

No one could stop Lionel and the Lepers.

One time, Newell's was in a tournament in Rosario that called for the champions to be awarded a prize— a new bicycle for each player. The Lepers always wanted to win a game, but this time they desperately wanted to win those bikes. As they warmed up, though, Lionel wasn't there. No one knew where he was. They kept looking around, expecting him to show up, but there was no sign of him. They knew Lionel wouldn't miss a game, let alone the championship game, with a new bicycle on the line. Yet as it started, no Lionel. Where was he?

Locked in his bathroom, it turns out. Lionel had accidently gotten stuck in the bathroom of his house. None of his family were home at the time.

No matter how much he banged and shouted, there was no one to open the door. As he realized he was going to miss the game, he did what he had to do—he broke the window and climbed out.

By the time he came sprinting to the field near his house where the game was being played, it was already halftime and Newell's was losing 2–0. The other team thought they might win the bicycles. Messi told his teammates what happened and they all laughed. He then assured them there was nothing to worry about. As the second half started, he quickly scored three times. Newell's won the title, and Lionel and all his teammates got their new bikes.

Another time, Lionel was sick for a game and couldn't play. Despite feeling terrible, he sat on the bench to cheer on his teammates. Newell's was soon in danger of losing, trailing 1–0. No matter how hard his teammates tried, they couldn't score to save their lives. Finally, with just a few minutes remaining, the coach looked down the bench at Lionel and asked if he thought he could manage enough energy to play the rest of the game. Lionel jumped at the chance. "Win me the game," the coach told Lionel, and sure enough, the young star scored two goals in the final minutes to deliver the Lepers another victory.

When Lionel and his teammates turned eleven, they moved to a bigger field and began playing traditional 11v11 soccer. That did nothing to slow them down. Lionel's ball control and passing ability turned the team into a high-powered offense. With more space to work with, Lionel felt like there was endless room to either pass to a teammate or dribble in and score himself. The offense was unstoppable, and in some games, the Newell's goaltender would lean against the post or sit down due to boredom.

"He was explosive," one of his youth coaches, Adrian Coria, told the author Luca Caioli. "He had a command that I had never seen on a football pitch . . . One-on-one he'd make mincemeat of you. He dominated the ball, always on the ground, always glued to his foot. He left behind all the big boys who still didn't have good control and movement."

One time, in search of talented competition, they traveled all the way to Lima, Peru, for an international tournament. It was an exciting trip. The smooth, well-manicured fields sparkled green, a far cry from the worn, mostly dirt pitches they were used to in Argentina. Many of the top youth teams from South America were there. Maybe now, everyone thought, the Machine of '87 would be challenged.

Spoiler alert: They weren't. The Lepers barreled to the finals and then won the championship courtesy of a 10–0 blowout. Lionel had five goals in the first half and eight for the game. The crowd in Peru couldn't believe their eyes.

As the Legend of Lionel and the Machine of '87 spread, opponents began to try to bully the star player. Lionel was still small, so defenders would try to knock him down, slam him, and kick him. If they couldn't catch him and his magical dribbles, then they would try to beat him up and intimidate him. It didn't work. Lionel was soft-spoken, but that didn't mean he wasn't tough.

"Even though the ball was bigger than him, he was never afraid," former teammate Sergio Maradona (not to be confused with Diego Maradona) told *Bleacher Report* years later. "He never cried. He played better when they kicked him. He was always brave. He wanted to play with the ball, to dribble, to go forward."

Another time, an opponent tried to talk trash and question just how good Lionel was. Lionel just smiled. "In one maneuver, Messi nutmegged him twice," then teammate Franco Falleroni told *Bleacher Report*. "Can you imagine? In the same play—two nutmegs! The boy stopped talking then."

Messi's dominance wasn't just due to his talent. During his years with Newell's, he also impressed coaches and teammates with his work ethic and almost singular focus on soccer. All he wanted to do was play soccer, practice soccer, and think soccer. He took everything about soccer seriously. He would use a brush to clean his cleats after every practice. He took time to tape his ankles before games to guard against sprains when getting kicked.

Lionel constantly trained. He took extra shots after practice. He dribbled a ball everywhere he could. And when he was alone or stuck inside his house, he tried to hone his footwork. He could soon juggle a ball hundreds of times without losing control. He'd do it for hours each night, slowly hard-wiring the muscle memory that made controlling the ball in a game seem effortless. When he got tired of juggling a ball, he moved to other objects—rolled-up towels or socks or even food, especially lemons and oranges. Soon he could use his feet and knees to tap those in the air for what felt like endless periods of time.

Lionel's skills became legendary. He would sometimes entertain fans during halftime by juggling for the entire fifteen minutes or do it while climbing up and down the stairs in the stands. To make money, he would perform in plazas as the public put coins in his hat. At that tournament in Peru, he was encouraged by his teammates to juggle for a crowd while they kept count.

"I think he got up to 1,200 touches," his coach at Newell's told *The Guardian*. "He was nine years old."

As passionate as he was about soccer, Lionel was a disinterested student. He was extremely shy and struggled to speak during class. Both his parents were educated, though, so they stressed schoolwork. He did what he needed to do to get by, but he mostly dreamed of soccer, replaying ways that he could have handled game situations.

"He thought like a professional," youth teammate Bruno Milanesio told *Bleacher Report*. "He had this conviction, this passion. He is crazy about football. He has been since he was very young. He thought all the time about the ball, how to dribble [past] other players, how to solve a situation. Every day, he trained to be better. He always wanted more, more, more. He put football before everything."

As fast and quick as Lionel was on the pitch, he was as slow and predictable off it. He slept constantly. He would get to bed early and rise late, sleeping ten hours a night. Then he'd nap after practice and even doze off in school. He walked slowly through the hallways. He even ate his meals slowly.

His sluggish pace was so well-known among his community that one year his teachers gave him a part in the school play that best represented his personality—a snail.

No one could understand how someone who whipped around the soccer field the way he did had so little energy for anything else.

One of the reasons, though, would change Lionel Messi's life.

4

Growth

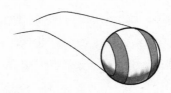

AT THE AGE OF NINE, Lionel Messi stood about four foot one, quite short for his age. More concerning, he had stopped growing. He had always been small, but as his teammates and opponents continued to get taller, he stayed the same height.

You don't have to be tall to be a soccer player. The game is as much about skill and smarts as it is physical power. Pelé, the Brazilian many consider the greatest player of all time, is just five foot eight. Diego Maradona is just five foot five. Some people believe being short can actually help a player—they have a lower center of gravity and their feet can be extremely coordinated.

"I think being smaller than the rest allowed me to be a bit quicker and more agile," Lionel told *The Guardian*.

Doctors, however, were now projecting Lionel to top out at just four foot eleven. That was concerning not just for soccer but for his general health as an adult. The lack of height also didn't make sense. No one else in his family was considered short, let alone abnormally short. They were of average size or bigger, including his parents and brothers. His younger sister was actually quite tall for her age.

In examining Lionel, a doctor in Rosario, Diego Schwarzstein, discovered the cause for his problem— he suffered from a growth hormone disorder. It affects about one out of every 20 million people. It delayed Lionel's bone age and thus slowed his growth. It was a mild form of dwarfism, the condition that stunts development.

The good news was Dr. Schwarzstein believed he had a cure. The bad news was it required daily injections of somatotropin, a growth hormone, via a needle. While getting a shot every day is generally a terrifying concept, Lionel was willing to do it. He considered it part of the process. If this would help him grow and become a professional soccer player, then he would endure the needles. He had just one question for Dr. Schwarzstein.

"Will I grow?" Lionel asked, according to ESPN.

"You will be taller than Maradona," Dr. Schwarzstein answered.

That was enough for Lionel. He learned to administer the injections himself. It was painful. But Lionel suffered through it bravely. He even began carrying a small blue cooler filled with needles so he would never miss a dose.

"Every night I had to stick a needle into my legs, night after night after night, every day of the week, and this over a period of three years," Lionel told *The Telegraph*. "I was so small, they said that when I went onto the pitch, or when I went to school, I was always the smallest of all."

Lionel combined the injections with even more sleep, which helped promote cell regeneration. He began taking naps after training, often just lying down in his uniform on the couch, a habit he continued into adulthood.

As much as Lionel hated the needles and the treatments and the doctors, he liked the results. He began to slowly grow taller and stronger. He was still small by almost any standards, but there was now hope he would overcome his condition.

The treatments were expensive, though, over $1,000 a month, which, due to the standard of living in Argentina and Lionel's father's salary at the time, was a huge sum of money. At first, the steel factory where Lionel's dad worked picked up most of the tab. The rest came from the health care provided by the Argentine government. Then an economic downturn hit the country when Lionel was about twelve and both sources of funding for the medicine ended. The family didn't have the money to afford the somatotropin on their own. The treatments would have to be discontinued.

The family was desperate for help and decided to ask Newell's Old Boys to pay. After all, if Lionel grew to his potential, then the club would benefit by having a great player. Newell's agreed. At least initially. Then, as the payments for the medicine mounted, they began to back off. Newell's wasn't a wealthy club. Spending so much money on a kid who was still years away from the men's professional team, and with no guarantee to even make it, was risky.

"They said, 'we will pay for the treatment, don't worry,'" Lionel's dad, Jorge, told *The Guardian*. "But it was like begging."

Jorge grew frantic. He needed to find a way to pay for the treatments. His son was courageously administering injections and doing everything he could to grow. But without money, Lionel's career was at risk.

They began working with a sports agent, Fabian Soldini, who they hoped could use his contacts in Argentina and abroad to find a solution. A tryout with a team in Buenos Aires impressed the coaches, but, like Newell's, they didn't have enough money to pay for the treatments.

The Messis concluded they'd have to look outside their home country for a solution, particularly in Europe. To get Lionel noticed, Fabian filmed him not just playing soccer but also juggling oranges and tennis balls over and over as a way to stand out from other scouting videos.

Fabian knew another agent, Josep Maria Minguella, who was highly respected. Back in the 1980s, he had represented Diego Maradona. Major clubs in Europe trusted him when he pitched South American players for tryouts.

Josep was particularly connected with Barcelona, one of the most famous and wealthiest teams in the world. It's won dozens of championships not just in Spain but across Europe. It's been home to some of the greatest players and managers of all time. The club counts millions of fans around the globe. If there was ever a soccer team that could afford Lionel's medical treatments, FC Barcelona was it.

Josep normally represented eighteen- or nineteen-year-olds, grown men who had proven they were ready to play at the top level of soccer, not twelve- or thirteen-year-olds. Even the greatest thirteen-year-old was a risk, and even if he did continue to develop, he was still five or six years away from becoming a professional.

So Fabian had to convince Josep to take a chance. He sent him a video of Lionel. Josep saw a level of skill that left him speechless. He had been coaching and scouting soccer since 1969 and he had never seen someone so young who was so talented and polished. The video even showed Lionel juggling an orange about 120 times. (Years later the footage would be used in a credit card commercial.) Josep decided to call Fabian. He was still skeptical.

Was this for real? Josep asked his old acquaintance. Was Lionel Messi legit? He was still a boy, after all.

Fabian promised he was, that as wild as this looked and sounded, Josep wouldn't regret putting his reputation on the line and convincing Barcelona to give a thirteen-year-old a tryout.

With nothing more than a video and Fabian's word, Josep Maria Minguella, one of the most powerful sports agents in soccer, decided to take the risk. He knew Barça would never sign Lionel without seeing him train and play. So Josep laid out thousands of dollars for flights and hotel rooms to bring Fabian, Jorge, and, of course, Lionel to Spain.

There were no guarantees, but Lionel Messi was headed out in the world to prove to everyone he was neither too young nor too small to achieve greatness.

5

La Masia

ON SEPTEMBER 16, 2000, Lionel stood in an airport in Argentina, about to board a flight with his father to Europe. He was crying.

The decision to travel to Spain and try to convince Barça to sign him at the age of thirteen had not come easily. While his dad was coming with him, he was leaving his mother, his younger sister, and his brothers back home, not to mention cousins, friends, teammates, classmates, and his old neighborhood and old school. The tryout could take a week or even weeks. If it was successful, Barcelona would become his new home. Life in Rosario would have to go on without him.

This journey was critical, intimidating, emotional, and scary all at the same time. His life, one way or the other, was about to change drastically.

In a couple of days, Lionel was scheduled to report to Barça's youth academy, which is called "La Masia," or "The Farmhouse." Because of his time with Newell's Old Boys, Lionel was familiar with the idea of a soccer academy. The ones in Argentina, though, were like well-organized youth travel teams. This was another level altogether.

The players at La Masia are some of the best in all of Spain. Many of them had joined La Masia when they were between six and eight years old. As many as a thousand kids try out each year. Those who make the team are the best of the best at that age. By the age of thirteen, they have had years of world-class training.

La Masia is more than just a soccer pitch. It is a complex. It includes a five-story building plus training grounds, fields, locker rooms, and cafeterias. There is also a dormitory to house players who are not from Barcelona and thus can't commute to the academy from their parents' home.

It is a serious place, but for a soccer-loving kid, it is also paradise. The day begins with breakfast at seven thirty. Then boys (there are no girls) attend a local school from eight a.m. to two p.m. From four p.m. to six p.m., there is training. Then they hit the gym for weight lifting or other workouts. At nine p.m. they all eat dinner together before lights-out at ten p.m. In their downtime the kids do homework, watch movies, listen to music . . . or often just play soccer in the dorm. While academics are stressed, this is a life built around soccer, soccer, and more soccer.

It costs FC Barcelona over $5 million a year to run La Masia, but the club believes it allows them to find top talent early and train them in what they call the "Barcelona Way." The club believes in having players with great technical ability (dribbling, first touches, passing) who can play multiple positions and move fluidly around the field. Less than one in ten kids who enroll in La Masia eventually make the main Barça club.

This was one of, if not the, finest and most competitive soccer schools in the world. And now Lionel Messi was there to prove he, this short kid from Rosario, Argentina, could make it.

Trying out for any team is nerve-racking. Every player wants to perform their best and show the coaches their full potential. Lionel had to wonder if he was good enough. Sure, he'd dominated in Argentina and elsewhere in South America, but did he have what it takes to compete against the top of the top? What if all these top kids from Europe were better? That was the normal pressure.

The entire tryout was strange to begin with. Barça just didn't sign thirteen-year-old foreigners. Every other thirteen-year-old at La Masia was from Spain. Even if Lionel made it as a foreigner, he wouldn't be eligible to play for the top Barcelona team in his age group for at least a year because league rules called for Spanish players only.

Worse for Lionel, it wasn't enough for him to show he was as good as them, or even a little bit better, in order to make the team. He couldn't even be just the best one there. He had to be the best at La Masia by a lot, so much better than everyone else that the club simply had to invest in him. Anything less, anything other than looking like the best thirteen-year-old in the world, and they could save money by simply not taking him. There was plenty of great young talent in Spain.

To commit to Lionel, Barça would need to take on more than just the cost of the growth hormone treatments. Lionel's father was adamant that if Lionel made the team, he would stay with him in an apartment with the family, not in the La Masia dormitory. While many young players do stay there, they are from Spain and are more comfortable in that surrounding. Lionel had just arrived in the country and knew no one. And while Spanish is spoken in both Spain and Argentina, many words and pronunciations are different, especially in the Catalonia region, where Barcelona is located.

That meant Lionel and his father would need to be set up in an apartment and the club would have to help his father find a job in Barcelona, which, due to immigration law and work visas, was a challenge unto itself. None of this was cheap.

Essentially, Barça would have to spend a lot of money and jump over a lot of hurdles just to sign a thirteen-year-old who, no matter how good he might be, was still no guarantee to make the main club one day because so many things can happen in a player's development.

Simply put, Lionel had to be amazing. That's the enormous pressure Lionel was under. And he knew it as he landed in Barcelona, a city of 1.6 million that sits on the Mediterranean Sea in the northeast part of Spain. The region is known for its beaches, its art, its architecture, and, of course, its soccer. Considered one of the most vibrant and prettiest cities in the world, it was like no place Lionel had ever seen, certainly not in Argentina. As he stared at the high rises scraping the sky during his taxi ride from the airport, it felt overwhelming.

Within a day of arriving, Lionel walked onto La Masia's training pitch for his first practice, his future hanging in the balance. As had become custom, the other players looked at this new kid from South America and scoffed at his size. They assumed the coaches had made a terrible error.

"That day when Leo arrived, and we saw how small he was, how skinny he was, we thought we were going to eat him," Marc Pedraza, a player there that day, told *Bleacher Report*.

And, as had also become custom, opinions changed once they started playing. In a scrimmage that first day, Lionel controlled the ball and the game, routinely humbling opponents with his skill, speed, and vision of the field.

"When he touched the ball, we saw that he was

a phenomenon," Pedraza said. "It was impossible to get the ball off him."

"You could see that the ball was attached to Messi's foot like a claw," Xavi Llorens, a Barça coach at the time, told *Bleacher Report* years later. "He was very fast, and he ran with his head down. It looked like it was impossible that he knew where he was going, but like Maradona, he had that panoramic vision. His head turned rapidly. He could see the play in advance."

Lionel scored five goals that day. A sixth was disallowed, which bothered Lionel. His father, in an effort to further motivate him, had told Lionel earlier that if he scored six goals at practice he'd buy him a new warm-up outfit that Lionel wanted. Lionel thought the disallowed goal was going to cost him, but his father was so proud he decided it should count. Lionel got his new gear.

The only problem was that soccer-wise, no one at the tryout had the authority to even sign Lionel. All of the coaches and scouts on hand were impressed, but only the team's technical director, Carles Rexach, could make the final decision.

Unfortunately for Lionel, Rexach wasn't in Barcelona at the time. He was in Australia, scouting older players at the 2000 Summer Olympics. He did keep hearing from everyone back home about Lionel Messi, Lionel Messi, Lionel Messi. But he wouldn't be back for seventeen days. Lionel's dad grew frustrated. Each day Lionel would go to La Masia and perform brilliantly. And yet there was no commitment. He didn't know who to trust or whether they should try to find another club or just go back to Argentina.

Finally, Rexach returned. A scrimmage was set up that afternoon, just for him to scout Lionel. This was, perhaps, the most important game of Lionel's life. He didn't just desperately want to make the team—he needed to make the team. Anything less and he was back to square one.

Carles Rexach arrived at the La Masia pitch just as the game began. Rexach was born and raised in Barcelona. He played on Barça's youth teams and later seventeen seasons on the Barça senior club. He was also a member of the Spanish National Team and then coached for decades at all levels of the sport. There was no questioning his ability to judge talent.

As the game started, Rexach walked up to one corner of the pitch. He began walking down the far sideline, before wrapping around one of the nets and eventually arriving at the benches, where the coaches and other team officials were. That's where he was supposed to watch the game with his assistants and make a judgment on Lionel.

As he walked, he watched Lionel play. Rexach's eyes nearly popped out of his head as he saw this wunderkind. In all his decades around the game, all the playing, all the training, all the coaching and scouting, he'd never seen anything like the Flea whipping around the field.

It took him only a few minutes to get all the way around the field and reach the coaches' bench. Once he arrived, he didn't settle in to compare notes or concentrate on the rest of the game. He had a single message for his assistants. They could end the game. He'd seen enough already.

"You can sign him up," Rexach said.

6

The Napkin

SIGNING LIONEL turned out to be more complicated than just getting Carles Rexach's approval. There were still issues to iron out. Following the tryout, Lionel and his father returned to Rosario, waiting to receive word from La Masia, but what they thought would be a quick process stretched across a couple of months. Barça wasn't giving up on Lionel, but even though Carles Rexach was sold on Lionel's potential, some members of the club's board of directors were still concerned about spending so much money on such a young player from the other side of the world.

Eventually, tales of Lionel's play at La Masia spread around Spain. Other clubs and scouts began to hear about this super-talent from Argentina who could magically dribble through defenders. With each retelling of the story, Lionel sounded better and better. He weaved through three players. Or was it five? Or was it the whole team? Everyone wanted to see for themselves.

Word even reached a club called Real Madrid. The word "Real" stands for "Royal" and is used by many soccer clubs. Real Madrid is Barcelona's hated rival in La Liga. The two teams have battled for over a century and any game between the two is called "El Clásico" or "The Classic."

El Clásico games can turn bitter between players and coaches. Fans have been known to fight in the stands. Each club is obsessed with not just getting better, but trying to prevent the other from improving as well. In a book about the history of Spanish soccer, author Phil Ball notes, "they hate each other with an intensity that can truly shock the outsider." You think the Yankees–Red Sox rivalry is heated? Well, Madrid vs. Barça might just be on another level entirely.

Real Madrid was like Barça in one sense: It was a

very wealthy team and thus could package a deal that would bring Lionel and his family to its youth academy. When Real Madrid heard that Barça was about to sign some unknown Argentine thirteen-year-old, it suddenly became interested in meeting Lionel Messi also, if only to prevent Barça from getting a great player. Suddenly, Lionel found himself in the middle of one of the biggest rivalries in sports.

Meanwhile, back in Barcelona, Rexach knew that if Lionel ever stepped on Real Madrid's training pitch, they would see the same talent he did. If that happened, they might sign him immediately, providing the medical treatment, a job for Lionel's dad, an apartment, and who knows what else. Rexach couldn't risk it. If Real Madrid stole Lionel away and Lionel became the star Rexach believed he might become, then Lionel would be scoring goals not for Barça but against it . . . and Rexach would go down in history as the guy who let Lionel Messi get away.

"We have to sign this kid right now," Rexach recalled thinking to *The Guardian.*

On December 14, 2000, Rexach had lunch with Horacio Gaggioli, who was serving as Lionel's agent. Gaggioli was there to inform Rexach that after months of inaction, Barça's time was up. The family was going to pursue other opportunities, including Real Madrid. They couldn't wait any longer. Each month without a hormone treatment could hurt Lionel's potential.

"We'll go elsewhere," Gaggioli said in retelling the moment to reporters years later.

Rexach heard the news and rather than plead for more time, pulled a paper napkin out of a container on the table. He then took out a pen and wrote on it.

"I, Charly Rexach, in my capacity as technical secretary for FC Barcelona, and despite the existence of some opinions against it, commit to signing Lionel Messi as long as the conditions agreed are met."

It wasn't an official contract, of course. It was close, though. "I knew for sure that I couldn't let that kid slip through our fingers," Rexach said in the book *Messi*.

Once Rexach signed the napkin, the Barça board of directors were basically stuck. They too feared the threat of Real Madrid stealing Lionel out from under them, so Barça officially signed him to a real contract. The club would provide medical care, training, and education for Lionel; housing for the Messi family; and a job with the club for Lionel's father. His salary would be about $34,000 a year in current

American money. It was an incredible amount to spend on a thirteen-year-old prospect, no matter how good he seemed at his age.

Of course, that napkin is now considered the most famous napkin in the history of soccer. It is prominently displayed inside the FC Barcelona museum for fans to see.

"That piece of paper changed the modern history of the club," Gaggioli said.

With his present and future secured, Lionel could now shift his focus back to the thing he loved most—actually playing soccer. But now he was performing on a whole new pitch.

Each player at La Masia was trying to climb up through the ranks of the club. As kids, players were divided by birth year, just like in the United States. Eventually, the best were put onto Youth B, the lowest-level Barça team, in hopes of advancing to Youth A.

If a player excelled there, they could reach Barça C as they got into their upper teens. It was a lower-level professional team playing in the fourth division of La Liga, sort of like minor league baseball. This was still incredibly good soccer, but it was no player's desired final destination. Next came Barça B and then finally Barça A, the prized professional club where million-dollar salaries and worldwide attention awaited.

Because everyone at La Masia and across FC Barcelona was talented, and because playing time and promotions were so coveted, it wasn't easy to move up. There was no such thing as equal playing time or opportunity like there is in rec leagues. Players had to treat every moment of practice as a chance to prove themselves, not just to move up, but to not get replaced by someone below them. This was incredibly competitive.

For Lionel, the challenge was even greater. As a foreigner in Spain, the rules of the national league meant he couldn't play on the Youth A team that competed across the country and in prestigious tournaments. Instead, he had to start at the bottom and that meant Youth B. While that was the standard team for his age group, were it not for the league's restrictions, Lionel would have otherwise been on the A team given his ability and the club's commitment to him.

Making matters worse, by the time Lionel got settled in Barcelona, in March 2001, the B team was already in the middle of its season, so he had to find a way to mesh with a new group of kids without just taking someone's playing time and becoming unpopular. As good as Lionel was, all of the players were good and there was chemistry among them. Everyone else on the team was Spanish. Lionel was from Argentina and was so shy he barely spoke. Lionel, wearing a team-issued number 9 uniform, not his preferred and soon to be famous number 10, had to find his way if he wanted to not just survive but thrive.

The last thing he needed was another hurdle to overcome. But in a game on April 21, when he tried to cut an opposing player, Lionel got kicked hard. It wasn't the first or last time a defender tried to bully Lionel, but this one was particularly violent. Lionel's legs surged with pain as he writhed on the field. He was taken off and quickly diagnosed with a fractured left leg. Just as he was establishing himself with his new teammates at this new club in this new world, he was out for two months, stuck wearing a splint and doing rehab.

When he finally healed, he suffered another injury, tearing a ligament in his left ankle as he walked down some stairs. That set him back just a few weeks, but it caused concern within Barça's organization that Lionel Messi wasn't just small, he was fragile and injury prone. Had the club been tricked into signing a player who would never play for them?

Meanwhile, his family had a difficult time making Barcelona feel like home. Lionel needed to adapt to a new school, a slightly different language, and an unfamiliar situation. He was never that interested in education in the first place, but in Rosario he had friends who could help. Now he was just a quiet foreigner. He rarely even spoke to the other Barça players. As loud as his play on the field was, he was just as silent off it. He never knew what to say or when to say it.

"He would return to the dressing room, sit down in a corner, change, and leave without a word," teammate Victor Vázquez said in *Messi*.

The rest of the family struggled also. María, his little sister, was desperately homesick and uncomfortable in Spain. Then his mother was forced to return to Argentina when her sister got sick. That just increased the pressure and loneliness on everyone.

That summer, during a vacation back in Rosario, the family wondered if they should even return to

Spain in the fall. So far, the experience had been somewhat of a disaster and everyone was unhappy. Maybe they should all just stay here in Argentina, with their friends and loved ones, and have Lionel return to Newell's Old Boys?

Lionel didn't agree. He believed he just needed to get healthy. He truly loved La Masia and the complete focus on soccer, despite missing his old life, friends, and school.

The family decided to temporarily split. Lionel and his father would return to Barcelona. Everyone else would remain in Rosario, where life was better for them. An ocean would separate them, but they'd do whatever it took to allow Lionel to succeed. Being away from his mother, sister, and brothers was heartbreaking at times for Lionel, who was by then fourteen years old.

There was one good bit of news during this difficult period. Barça's doctors and trainers determined that Lionel no longer needed growth hormone shots. Instead, they believed a strict regimen of diet and exercise, including lots of sleep, would be enough from this point on. Lionel was now almost five foot three and while he was still the shortest player on the team, the doctors said his growth plates were still open and he would continue to gain inches naturally.

By February 2002, about a year after arriving at La Masia, things began to finally click. Lionel was able to establish Spanish residency, which allowed him to begin playing in international tournaments for Barça. In one critical game, he came on at halftime and scored three goals to lead his team to victory.

Lionel also began to feel more comfortable with his teammates. During trips to tournaments, he had no choice but to interact with them. They began to bond through video games, passing the hours in hotels competing in PlayStation soccer games. Lionel, his teammates would learn, was just as competitive playing video games as he was out on the pitch.

Mostly, though, Lionel focused on his training. At La Masia, he learned to be more than just a great dribbler. His coaches taught him to be a complete player, capable of seeing beyond the next individual move.

"[Lionel was] very receptive, always attentive to everything, quiet, shy, reserved with great class," his coach at the time, Alex Garcia, said in *Messi*. "He was conscious of the fact that he had an opportunity at Barça. He knew what it meant to make a sacrifice—

both his sacrifice and his family's. He didn't want to waste the opportunity he had been given."

Lionel even accepted the La Masia tradition of playing kids out of position—making, say, natural scorers such as Lionel play on defense. The mission of La Masia was not just having a player be his best at age thirteen, but developing him into a far better player as a professional. That meant learning different strategies and techniques from various positions that might help him when he returned to his natural spot.

"I moved him all over the pitch so he could develop all of his skills," Coach Garcia said. "It was almost a given in the youth teams."

"I think he introduced us to the street football style, 'playground football,' as they say in Argentina," Coach Garcia said. "We, in turn, have tried to instill in him our attacking kind of football, the Barça kind—getting the ball a lot, playing as hard as we can, going forward in only two or three touches, driving the ball toward the center of the pitch and then pushing forward through the opposition's half."

The one thing that Lionel didn't have to improve on was his will to win. One time, going into the season finale, Lionel's team was on the verge of capturing the league championship. The problem? Lionel had broken his cheekbone during a collision in the previous match. Doctors said he would be out two weeks and would have to miss the game.

Instead, Lionel decided to borrow a clear protective mask that the club had made the year prior for one of the Barça A team players who had suffered a similar injury. That way he could help win the title. That mask, however, was designed for a grown man. Lionel was still a kid, so when the game started, the mask kept sliding down over his eyes and he couldn't see. After two minutes, he ran over to the bench and tossed the mask to Coach Garcia and tried to run back into the action.

Coach Garcia shouted to Lionel to stop. He couldn't let him continue and risk further injury.

"No," Lionel pleaded, according to Coach Garcia. "Please, Coach, leave me on just a little bit longer."

Coach Garcia was concerned but decided to give his star player a couple of minutes of action. Knowing his playing time was going to be limited, Lionel didn't waste a second. He quickly got the ball and dribbled around some defenders and the goalie to score. Then, moments later, he took a cross and made a beautiful finish. Coach Garcia pulled Lionel off soon after. Playing with a broken cheekbone and in danger of further injury, Lionel had made sure to set his team up for the league title.

"You've done enough for your team," Coach Garcia said. "You can rest on the bench now."

Lionel Messi was proving himself worthy of all that investment.

7

Barça Debut

IN 2003, Lionel Messi turned sixteen years old. A normal American teenager would be a sophomore or maybe a junior in high school. If they played soccer, perhaps they'd try out for their school's varsity team.

Lionel was ready to step onto the big stage.

He was now almost five foot seven. His build was still slight, like most teenagers, but his speed and quickness were incredible. He could dribble, shoot, and most importantly see plays develop ahead of time. All those lessons from La Masia were sinking in.

He quickly rose from the Youth B team to the Youth A team, for which he was now eligible. That brought stronger competition and more opportunity to play in elite tournaments across Europe. He proved right at home, scoring eighteen goals in his first eleven games.

One day in November 2003, Lionel was approached after practice by the academy team coordinator, Josep Colomer. Lionel thought Colomer wanted to discuss something about his Youth A team. Or maybe, at most, Colomer might mention Lionel moving up to Barcelona C, the next rung of the club's ladder. He'd still be young for Barça C, and he'd only been on Youth A for a brief time, but it was possible. Any promotion would have been a big deal for Lionel.

Colomer, however, wasn't there to discuss Barça C or even Barça B. He was there with a surprise. He told Lionel to pack his bags, he was going to travel to Portugal to play in a friendly with the main Barcelona team, Barça A.

"Colomer talked to me about a few things and then told me I would be traveling with the first team," Lionel recalled to an Argentine television station years later.

A friendly is just an exhibition match rather than an official game, and this was not a permanent move, but that didn't matter to Lionel. This was the top team, after all. This was where he wanted to be. In a matter of months, he had rocketed up through the club, from Youth B to the top team.

Lionel would be playing for Barcelona's coach, Frank Rijkaard, who had just taken over at Barça and was looking to build a champion. If he took a liking to Lionel's game, he had the power to make him a permanent member of the team.

Colomer's advice was very simple—just be yourself and don't get overwhelmed. He didn't want the pressure of trying to do too much, too soon to make Lionel so nervous he performed poorly. Nerves can affect every athlete, even near-unflappable Lionel Messi.

Colomer made it clear, no matter what happened—good or bad—it was just one game. Lionel was only sixteen. Everyone else on the pitch would be in their twenties or thirties. He was still considered a youth player. For now, at least.

"[Colomer] told me that I should just go and enjoy the game and the experience, but when I came back I should concentrate on the Youth A team," Lionel said.

But could Lionel really treat this like just another game?

He was well aware of the hardship and sacrifice it took for him to pursue this dream. His family was split up, living on opposite sides of the Atlantic, each member missing the others desperately as they tried to spread their money around so they could all survive.

Likewise, he knew the gamble that Barça had made on him, having paid a pretty penny to recruit this little Argentine Flea with lots of potential, but with no guarantees that the bet would pan out. He knew that so many coaches and scouts had put their reputations on the line to get him to La Masia.

And lastly, he knew the work he'd put in—the painful growth hormone shots, the endless training at La Masia, and the hours and hours of individual drills. And that didn't even factor in the courage it took for a painfully shy kid to attempt to make a name for himself in a whole new world.

He knew the last thing he needed to do was dwell on all of that baggage and blow his big chance to shine. He knew he needed to just be Lionel Messi. That's what got him here, after all.

"They said I should enjoy everything I was doing and that there was no reason to make any change," Lionel said. "I should just continue in the same way."

Lionel was just 16 years and 145 days old for the game in Portugal, the third youngest to ever play in a friendly for Barcelona. Sixteen-year-olds, even great ones, rarely play with top European clubs, with and against grown men and established stars. The atmosphere that night was electric for the game against Porto, one of Portugal's most successful pro teams. Some fifty thousand fans had come out for the first game in Porto's brand-new stadium and to see the famed Barça squad.

"November 16, 2003, is a very important date for me," Messi said later on Argentine TV. "Because that's when I was able to make my childhood dream come true. It was a very happy day for me. I'd fought hard to make that moment happen. It was really special."

Lionel started the game on the bench, taking it all in. The crowd. The players. The excitement. He was finally where he'd always dreamed he would end up. The training sessions leading up to the game had been exciting. So had the trip and surveying the huge crowd before the game. By the second half, as the minutes ticked away, Lionel still hadn't gotten to play and he wondered if he'd get called at all. If not, he'd be disappointed, but just being there would still count as a great experience.

Finally, seventy-five minutes into the contest, and with just fifteen minutes remaining, Coach Rijkaard sent him in. He wore a number 14 jersey that was a little baggy.

He immediately impacted the game, finding the ball on numerous occasions, showing his typical foot skills and driving hard to the net, as Barça's system prefers. In the eightieth minute, Lionel broke through the defensive line and accepted a pass just inside the top of the box. He was able to take a touch but a defender and the goalie closed fast, preventing him from getting a full shot on. Instead, he stabbed the ball toward the net. While it was easily blocked, it was a dangerous opportunity.

"I had a really good chance against the goalkeeper," Lionel said years later. "But I didn't get hold of it. [Coach] Rijkaard came up to me after the game and said that I missed the chance."

Minutes later, he used his tremendous speed and work ethic to disrupt the ball in the Porto defensive end. By pressuring a defender, Lionel forced a pass back to the goalkeeper. However, the defenseman's pass was soft, and Lionel swooped in and took control of it from the charging keeper. He pushed the ball wide and had an angle to either shoot or dribble to the net, but instead chose to cut back and try to find a teammate alone in space at the other end of the box. That pass was offline and the play went nowhere.

"I went out to try to do as well as I could and to try to score a goal," Lionel said. "I didn't see at the time how much space I had. I should have shot."

Indeed, he should have, but those decisions would come with experience. In the moment, he could be proud of the fact that he had created the opportunities with beautifully timed runs, effort, and skill. If anything, he'd played too unselfishly, which is a good problem to have. His dribbling held up against grown professionals. He clearly needed to get stronger because the Porto players repeatedly pushed him off the ball or knocked him down. But that's true of all sixteen-year-olds. More weight and muscle would come naturally.

Barça lost that day, 2–0, but there was an immediate buzz among Barça fans, teammates, and coaches about Lionel Messi, this young phenom.

"He only had fifteen minutes, but he played really well and he had two chances to score," Coach Rijkaard told the media after. "The future he has is promising."

When Lionel returned to La Masia, he was moved up to Barcelona C. It was a sign of what the club saw in him. He played ten games with the C team, scoring five goals, before being promoted to Barcelona B, the main reserve team. Everything was happening quickly.

He was again brilliant, pumping in goals. One time, he collected the ball at midfield, noticed the goalkeeper was too far off his end line, and hammered a long shot with a perfect arc toward the net, over the keeper's outstretched arm and just under the crossbar for an improbable goal. It was world class.

There was one assignment that made the Barça coaches and directors particularly proud of Lionel. In the spring of 2004, the Youth B team was in the final games of its season with a chance to win a league championship.

Lionel had moved onto bigger and better things by then. He was training mostly with the Barça B team and once a week with the Barça A team. His future was clear. Yet when asked if he would go back to his past and substitute for the last three contests of the Youth B season, he jumped at the chance. While many players would look down on returning to a lower level of soccer, or refuse because they didn't want to risk injury or exhaustion with the extra games, Lionel saw it differently.

First off, this was a chance to play and he always wanted to play. Second, these were his old teammates. He may have moved up quickly that year, but the bond was still there. And third, a championship is a championship.

His return was a success. He scored a critical goal that helped seal the title for Youth B. Then he and his teammates celebrated like they had won the World Cup.

Barça knew that, if nothing else, what they had in Lionel Messi was a competitor. Couple that with the skill they saw in those fifteen minutes of play in Porto and they were excited about the future for both Lionel and Barcelona.

"It seemed as if he had been playing with us all his life," Barça assistant coach Henk Ten Cate said of the Porto game. "His movement was so natural . . . If you are fifteen or sixteen in a game like that against Porto, at the opening of a new stadium full of people, and you do all that, it is because you are something special.

"[Coach Rijkaard] and I looked at each other, 'Did you see that?'"

Soon everyone would.

8

The Decision

LIONEL'S SOCCER CAREER was taking off. He was just sixteen and on the cusp of playing in La Liga.

While those early days in Barcelona had been lonely and confusing, after three years in Spain, he had grown more comfortable with his teammates and more familiar with the country. He now knew his way around Barcelona and understood the slang, accents, music, and culture. Due to his excellent play and continued hard work, he was presented a new contract, which while nowhere near as rich as ones to come, offered his family the financial security to live comfortably in both Europe and South America.

Yet Argentina never left his heart. It was still so deeply tied to his identity that one day, when he was approached with an important question, the answer came immediately.

In the spring of 2004, the coach of the Under 17 (U-17) Spanish National Team presented Lionel with an offer: "How would you like to play with us and join the Spanish national program?" This would be in addition to playing for Barça. In soccer, as with basketball, a player will have a professional team, but also represent his country in the Olympics and other tournaments during the off-season.

In international soccer, players generally play for their home country's national team and as teenagers begin participating in youth teams overseen by their national governing body. In the United States, that's US Soccer, which fields national sides as young as U-15.

Under the rules of FIFA, once a player steps onto the pitch for one national team, he or she is forever committed to that country. You can't play for, say, France for a few years and then switch to Canada, the way professional players can change teams.

This usually isn't a big deal. Most people are citizens of only one country and thus eligible for one team. However, some players have a choice. A child born to an American serving in the military who happened to be stationed on, say, a US Army base in Germany, would be eligible for both the United States and Germany. It's similar for a child born in America whose parents are immigrants from, say, Mexico. They can play for either country's national team.

It can get complicated, but essentially, FIFA says that if a player is eligible to get a passport from a country, then he or she is eligible to play for that country.

Lionel was a special case because he had moved to Spain at such a young age, before he was old enough to be eligible to play for the youngest level of the Argentina national program. Had he stayed in Rosario, he certainly would have been discovered and brought into the system. Instead, now he was sixteen and wasn't sure anyone back home even remembered him or knew that he was a rising talent.

After three years of living in Barcelona, in addition to some ancestry that was rooted back in Spain, Lionel was eligible to play for the powerful Spanish National Team.

Now he was being asked to choose—Argentina or Spain. His birth country versus his adopted home.

While Lionel saw himself as an Argentine, the Spanish offer was tempting. He assumed he'd eventually land on the Argentina National Team's radar and they'd recruit him, but in that moment, he had no guarantee.

Lionel also knew almost no elite players in Argentina anymore. He was friends with lots of Spanish prospects from La Masia, though. And it was a very strong group of players. In 2010, Spain would go on to win the World Cup, and its team featured nine La Masia players, all of whom were Lionel's friends. At this point, Lionel was more at home among the Spanish than the Argentines.

Yet if Lionel accepted the Spanish offer, he'd close that Argentine door forever and never wear the fabled white-and-light-blue vertical-striped jersey. He might, indeed, win a World Cup with Spain, but he'd never have a chance to follow in the footsteps of Diego Maradona and be a hero to the kids in Rosario, Buenos Aires, and elsewhere in Argentina. He knew what that team meant to his fellow countrymen back home, even if he no longer lived there. He grew up walking past those murals of

Maradona. He remembered the people in the market wearing their team jerseys. He knew the passion and pride of the homeland. And while Spain had a great team, Argentina had won the World Cup in 1978 and 1986. Perhaps, with Lionel leading the team, they could win it all again.

The decision, therefore, was easy. He immediately said, "no thank you" to the Spanish offer. He was an Argentinean, not a Spaniard.

"Not for a minute did I have any doubts," Lionel said years later. "It wouldn't have been the same."

Lionel assumed, correctly, that if he continued to progress as a player, especially if he made the Barcelona A team and began playing in the first division of La Liga, that word would get back to Argentina about him and he would be offered a spot in their national program. In fact, it didn't even take that long.

A man named Claudio Vivas was an assistant coach within the Argentina national system. He hailed from Rosario and had once played for Newell's Old Boys. While he was much older than Lionel and never directly coached him, he never forgot that young star of Newell's Machine of '87. Even after Lionel moved to Barcelona, Vivas made a habit of trying to keep up with his progress, if only out of curiosity and hometown pride.

As Lionel climbed the ranks at Barça, Vivas acquired footage of Lionel playing and then sent it around to the Argentine national coaches. They were immediately intrigued and tried to reach out to Lionel. They still knew little about him, and the first letter they sent him was addressed to "Leonel Mecci."

While Argentina didn't know how to spell his name, they did know they needed to get Lionel in a game as soon as possible. They scheduled two friendlies, or exhibition games, in June 2004 for Lionel to play for the U-20 national team. "We made it happen only for him," the manager of the team said to author Leonardo Faccio.

That would allow them to see Lionel in person while locking him in for Argentina. Even though Lionel had rejected Spain once, until he played for Argentina, he could always change his mind. Spain certainly hadn't stopped asking and pleading with him to play for them.

The first friendly was against Paraguay. Lionel arrived a few days early to train with his new team and he found himself in a familiar position—as an outsider. This time the roles were reversed. When he'd first gone to Barcelona, he was a kid from Argentina. Now he was returning to Argentina as a kid from Barcelona. Even though he was from Rosario, he had been gone long enough that he knew none of the other players, who had spent the past few years training together and competing against one another.

He was a stranger in his own country, a shy introvert who was trying to fit in. At least he knew what to do, having learned from his early days at La Masia—let his play on the pitch do most of the talking for him. His teammates quickly realized what a talent he was and began dreaming of him joining their already promising team.

On June 29, five days after Lionel turned seventeen, he came off the bench for his first appearance for Argentina. Just getting to wear the famed kit of his country made it memorable. He couldn't count the number of nights he'd fallen asleep as a child dreaming of wearing the uniform. Now it was real. For good measure, he even scored a goal in the easy 8–0 victory.

Days later, in a 4–1 victory over Uruguay, he scored again. He also delivered four assists across the two games and dazzled everyone with his ability. Despite being the youngest player in the U-20 program, he was named to the team that would compete in the upcoming 2005 FIFA Under 20 World Cup.

"I loved him," the U-20 coach, Hugo Tocalli said in *Messi*. "I loved his change of pace from zero to a hundred in no time at all, his trick of dodging past his opponent, his ability to move extremely fast with the ball still glued to his foot. He demonstrated that despite his stature, he was able to score many goals."

The 2005 FIFA Under 20 World Cup was held in the Netherlands. While the U-20 World Cup generally lacks the fans and media attention of an actual World Cup, the intensity of the competition is basically the same. These are the best young players in the world, all trying to deliver glory for their country.

Lionel was excited. But then he did not start in the opening game against the United States. The coach's decision was puzzling. He eventually was subbed in, but keeping him off the field at all proved questionable when Argentina struggled to score and got upset by the Americans, 1–0.

Thankfully, the loss came in the first round, known as the "group stage," which wasn't single elimination. The knockout stages would begin in the next round, if Argentina made it that far.

Lionel remained positive, telling the media that he respected the decision and that "the team will pick up the pace because we have some good players." He knew they would need to play better immediately. Argentina arrived with high expectations, but if they were to suffer another loss, or perhaps just a draw, it might cause them to be eliminated. Suddenly, the pressure was considerable.

The next game was against Egypt and Lionel not only started, he scored the critical first goal of the game as Argentina cruised to a 2–0 victory. They then defeated Germany 1–0 to advance to the knockout stage. Now it was win or go home.

In the round of sixteen, Argentina matched up against South American rival Colombia, which was considered one of the favorites to win the Cup. Colombia took a 1–0 lead, which was concerning for Argentina because Colombia had breezed undefeated through group play without allowing even a single goal.

But then Lionel ended the Colombian defense's scoreless streak with a goal in the fifty-eighth minute, finishing a give-and-go by hammering a beautiful left-footed shot past the keeper. Then in extra time, the ninety-third minute, Argentina's Julio Barroso scored in dramatic fashion to move the team forward.

Up next in the quarterfinals . . . Spain, the very team that Lionel Messi could have chosen to play for, featuring a number of teammates from La Masia who he had lived, trained, and played with. They were like brothers to him at this point. That included Spanish midfielder Cesc Fabregas, who Lionel had been particularly close with when he first arrived at La Masia. For Lionel, this was personal. Not only was a U-20 World Cup potentially on the line, but so were bragging rights when he got back to Barcelona.

"I've got along well with Messi ever since the first day we met in the youth academy," Cesc told reporters. "I've spent three amazing years with him, scoring goals, doing two on ones. I've had a great time."

The game was tied 1–1 until the seventy-first minute, when Lionel assisted on a goal. With the score now 2–1 Argentina, he then followed up with a spectacular play where he plucked the ball out of the air with his first touch, then tapped it through the defense in the air to an open space. It was like a self-pass. He then chased the ball down and was in alone on the goalkeeper for a relatively easy finish. It's the kind of impossible maneuver only Lionel could make. It not only knocked Spain out of the tournament, but left them thinking about what they could have been if they had just convinced Lionel to play for them.

As big as playing Spain was for Lionel, the semi-final matchup was even bigger for Argentina—it was a face-off against archrival Brazil. The two South American countries share over seven hundred miles of border as well as an obsession with soccer. Historically, they are two of the most successful teams in the world. Brazil has captured five World Cups and Argentina two. Each country came into this contest with four previous U-20 World Cup titles. Fans constantly debate which nation is better at soccer, each boasting a slew of individual greats, including two of the greatest of all time, Maradona of Argentina and Pelé of Brazil.

Every player from each country is taught at a very young age that there is almost nothing more important than beating the other. ESPN has rated it the single greatest soccer rivalry in the world. Lionel may have been living in Spain the last few years, but he knew what this meant to his country. The fact that a spot in the finals was also on the line only added to the drama.

Any game between the two teams is followed closely by fans back home. Lionel's superb performances in the tournament thus far had increased his profile in Argentina, as newspapers and television reports introduced him to fans who now saw Lionel as their returning hero with the magical game. Almost immediately, fans and media began buzzing about how he might be the next Maradona, a star capable of leading Argentina to a World Cup.

It didn't take long for Lionel to leave his mark. Just seven minutes into the game, he collected a pass about thirty yards out from the net, on the right side. He was surrounded by four defenders but quickly made four small touches with his left foot to move into the slightest bit of space. He then unleashed a wicked shot with his left foot. It ripped in between two Brazilian defenders, past a diving goalkeeper, and into the upper right corner of the net.

It was an incredible goal, a combination of supreme talent and nerve. It was a gifted young star unafraid of the pressure of the game. All over Argentina, fans watching Lionel Messi for the first time were enthralled and overjoyed.

Brazil, unfazed and accustomed to pressure-filled matches against Argentina, tied it in the seventy-fifth minute. But during extra time, in the ninety-third minute, Lionel made another play, securing the ball on the left end line and passing it back into the box to a teammate, who knocked home the game winner. Lionel and his teammates swarmed one another in celebration. Brazil was beaten. Argentina rejoiced. Only one game separated Lionel and Argentina from a championship.

Nigeria awaited in the finals, but Lionel was prepared. In the fortieth minute of a scoreless game, Argentina was awarded a penalty kick. The Argentine coach told Lionel to take it. The coach hadn't started Lionel in the opener but by now had learned his lesson. This was the best player on the team. Lionel responded by calmly stepping to the penalty dot to take the shot.

While the stakes were high and the intensity of the competition incredible, he remained as calm as ever, like he was still a boy playing for fun in the streets of Rosario. He had long ago learned that remaining steady was one of the keys to a penalty kick. He would simply choose a spot in the net where he wanted the ball to go, and consider it less of a shot and more of a pass to that specific location. Many penalty kicks fail when the shooter tries to do too much or grows too nervous. They wind up hitting it too hard and thus off target.

Lionel wouldn't allow that to happen. He easily knocked the ball into the lower left corner to give Argentina the lead.

Nigeria didn't get to the finals by accident, though, and they soon tied the game. Then, in the seventy-fifth minute, it happened again. An Argentine player was fouled in the box and the team was awarded another penalty kick. Once again Lionel, the youngest kid on the team, was told to take it. And once again he remained relaxed and cracked it into the net, this time low to the right.

It proved to be the tournament winner, as Lionel and his teammates soon hoisted the cup. His six goals were the most scored in the tournament and he was named the event's best player.

Back in Argentina, every soccer fan now knew his name.

9

Stardom

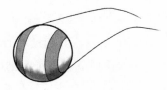

PRIOR TO THE 2005 U-20 World Cup, on October 16, 2004, Lionel had made his official La Liga debut for Barcelona, running into a league game against Espanyol FC in the eighty-second minute. While he didn't score, he became, at the time, the youngest to ever play for Barça in an official game (not merely a friendly). He was just seventeen years, three months, and twenty-two days old.

In America, he'd have still been in high school.

Across the 2004–05 season, Lionel would get seventy-seven minutes of playing time as a substitute in nine games. Barça had quickly become a La Liga power under Coach Rijkaard, winning the league title for the first time in six seasons. On a team that talented, playing time was tough to earn. Lionel did impress his teammates, though, who began to suggest to coaches that he deserved more opportunity on the field.

On May 1, 2005, Lionel got into a game late against Albacete. Within minutes, he fielded a pass over the defensive line from the Brazilian Ronaldinho, who was a star of the team. Lionel brought the ball down with one touch of his left foot. Now alone with the charging goalkeeper, he calmly chipped it over the keeper's head and into the net for what appeared to be his first-ever Barça goal.

Yet before he could celebrate, he heard whistles. A teammate was called offside. It was a beautiful, technically brilliant play, but it was all for naught. Even the Albacete keeper playfully patted Lionel on the head, a sign of how nice a shot that was and, perhaps, a way of letting the kid know that he shouldn't worry—the goals would come.

Indeed, they would. Quickly. Rather than lingering in his disappointment, Lionel kept working. Just minutes later, nearly the same scenario unfolded.

Ronaldinho tapped a ball high toward Lionel, who let it bounce and then chipped it over a sliding defender and the fast-approaching keeper. It was nearly the same play.

But with one major difference—this time there was no whistle, just excitement as Lionel jumped for joy and hugged Ronaldinho and the others. He was, at the time, the youngest player to ever score a goal for Barça.

"I really enjoyed it," Lionel said after.

It would be his only goal of the 2004–05 season, but there was no denying what he meant to the club. He was soon signed to a contract that would keep him in Barcelona until at least 2014.

Each Barcelona season runs from roughly August to June and is broken into three distinct competition segments. Unlike in American sports, a professional soccer team in Europe will compete in more than one league.

For Barça, there is La Liga, the main professional league in Spain. There is also the Copa del Rey, which is a separate knockout tournament involving Spanish teams. And finally there is the Champions League, which is a competition among the best professional teams from all of the European leagues, including the British Premier League, Bundesliga in Germany, and so on. Winning that is a tremendous accomplishment, the best of the best.

Despite suffering a torn hamstring that limited him to twenty-five appearances in 2005–06, Lionel managed to score eight goals. In a stretch in January and February 2006, he scored six in seven games. He was still just eighteen years old, but he began to fit in, and at times even dominate, on a power-house Barcelona club that won La Liga and, most impressively, its second-ever Champions League title by defeating Arsenal of the British Premier League in the final.

His teammates quickly became believers in his talent. A great example of their support came in 2005, when Ronaldinho won the coveted Ballon d'Or, which is awarded to the world's best player. He had been the most productive player for Barça's rise to success as well as the leader of the Brazilian national team. He deserved to win. Yet he used the opportunity to warn everyone of what was about to come from his young teammate that he battled against in practice. Maybe he was getting the award, but Lionel was on his mind.

"This award says I'm the best player in the world, but I'm not even the best player at Barcelona," Ronaldinho said. Some in the media thought he was joking or just being humble, but Ronaldinho said he was telling the truth. "Someday I will explain that I was at the birth of one of the footballing greats: Leo Messi."

With those monumental expectations on his shoulders, Lionel continued to up his game, scoring seventeen goals in 2006–07, including six goals in Barça's final four games. He would score sixteen more the following season. He was also winning a reputation for scoring in the most important moments, capitalizing on his ability to shrug off pressure.

On March 10, 2007, with Lionel's career on the rise, Barça hosted Real Madrid, their hated rival, in the latest El Clásico match. The game always attracts additional attention, from the supporters desperate for victory, to the larger than normal media contingent, to the coaches and staff of both clubs. It took place in front of 97,823 fans at Camp Nou, Barça's legendary home stadium.

And it went something like this. Madrid took a 1–0 lead in the fourth minute. Lionel tied it in the tenth. Madrid took a 2–1 lead in the twelfth minute. Lionel tied it in the twenty-seventh. Madrid took a 3–2 lead in the seventy-second minute, and the game, which would feature eight yellow cards and incredibly physical play, seemed over as the minutes ticked away.

Then Lionel got the ball in the eighty-eighth minute, cut through three defenders and into the box, and slammed a shot back across the goal and into the net to secure the 3–3 tie. He'd scored a hat rick, the first of over fifty he would score in his career, and all three of his team's goals on the day.

The crowd sang "Messi, Messi, Messi" at the result, yet Lionel could be only so happy. "It would have been nicer if we had won," he said.

Each game he seemed to display some new, awe-inspiring move that won him more fans, not just in Barcelona or even across Spain but around the world. His skills, moves, and dribbling ability were watched and studied everywhere via the Internet. Television audiences for Barça grew.

In Barcelona, the media called him "Messiah" and soon, just as Ronaldinho predicted, he became the star of the team.

He had also finally grown into his frame and

began a dedicated regime of fitness and weight lifting to build strength. His diet was strict, full mostly of vegetables, fish, and chicken. Sweets of any kind were forbidden. Lionel always liked to sleep, but now he prioritized it, believing rest was a key to preventing injuries.

In 2007, the year he turned twenty, he finished third in voting for the Ballon d'Or. In 2008, he was the runner-up. In those two years he combined to score fifty-three total goals for Barça and Argentina.

This was also a time when Lionel changed his number. At the start of his Barça career, he had worn number 30 before switching to number 19. At the time, Ronaldinho wore number 10, but as he got older, his career stalled and he decided to play in Italy. Ronaldinho had always been supportive of Lionel. He was never jealous of his talent or the way fans flocked to him. Rather, Ronaldinho was an ideal teammate and mentor, helping Lionel transition to a first team superstar.

"[Ronaldinho] was a great help," Messi told Barça TV. "It's never easy to go into a changing room at the age of sixteen especially with my [shy] character."

Ronaldinho decided that if he was going to leave

Barça, then he wanted his young Argentinian friend to take his jersey.

"He had it in his mind that he was leaving and he told me to have his number," Lionel told Barça TV.

The number 10 is significant in soccer. Traditionally, players on the field were assigned a number based on their position. It started from the back, with goalkeepers wearing number 1, defenders numbers 2 through 5, and so on. Through the years, and various formations, the number 10 position was left to creative, high-scoring forwards, such as Lionel. Those players are often the most exciting player on a team and thus attract the most fans. Famous number 10s include both Pelé and Maradona. More kids grow up dreaming of wearing number 10 than any other number.

Ronaldinho understood that Lionel could be the next great number 10 in soccer. His game was that good. For the 2008–09 Barça season, the switch was made and Lionel's number 10 jersey, in the club's famed blue and red, became one of the bestsellers in the world. That same year, Lionel began wearing the number 10 on Argentina's equally famous sky-blue-and-white jerseys.

By this point, Lionel was being paid nearly $9

million a year to play soccer, but was also reaping endorsement money. Every global company seemingly wanted to be associated with this star who, despite speaking so few words and granting so few interviews, had captured the imagination of fans, particularly young fans, around the globe.

His chief sponsor was Adidas, which featured him in dozens of commercials and regularly produced signature shoes and soccer boots featuring his name. He also had major deals with Pepsi, EA Sports, Gillette, and many more.

He enjoyed making commercials and even found a way to turn them into a competition. For one such advertisement, he was asked to dribble a ball and then shoot it off the crossbar of the goal, have it come right back to him, and then hit it off the crossbar again, and then do it a third time. It would make for a cool video but was an incredibly difficult request.

"Can you do it?" the director of the commercial asked Lionel according to author Leonardo Faccio.

"What are we betting?" Lionel asked.

The director wasn't expecting such a question. Lionel was already being paid to be in the commercial, but if this would motivate him, then they would bet. The director was concerned it would take hours to get the proper shot. Maybe this would speed things up. An offer was made. Lionel would get twenty cases of soda, a rare treat Lionel occasionally allowed himself to have, if he could hit the crossbar three times in a row. Lionel agreed.

On the first try, Lionel hit the crossbar twice, but the ball got away on the third attempt. On the next try, he hit the crossbar fourteen times in a row. He'd won the bet but wasn't satisfied. He grabbed the ball, and with the camera rolling, hit it twenty consecutive times.

With that, Lionel won his soda.

In another commercial, Lionel was asked to leap in the air and scissor kick a ball through a pane of glass, shattering it for effect. To do it properly for the camera, he needed to hit a very small red dot in the middle of the glass. When he missed on the first attempt, Lionel saw a production assistant scowl. Upset at being doubted, he hit the dot perfectly on his next attempt, busting the glass everywhere. He then had them bring out another plate of glass, and he hit the red dot with the ball again, smashing the glass all over the place. What could have been a long day of filming was over quickly.

Lionel was now making as much money through endorsements as he was playing soccer. For a kid who had grown up with little in Rosario, his world had changed dramatically.

There was one thing that didn't change, though. At that stage of his career, Lionel reconnected with a girl he had known since he was very young, Antonella Roccuzzo. She was the sister of one of Lionel's friends and soccer teammates growing up in Rosario, Lucas Scaglia.

While Lionel was in Spain and focused on his soccer career, Antonella attended college in Argentina. When they met again during one of Lionel's vacations back to Rosario, they began dating. Lionel has always liked to keep a small circle of friends, most of whom knew him long before he became a star. Antonella fit into that. Lionel spent much of his childhood hanging around her house, playing with Lucas. He and Antonella had known each other nearly their entire lives. He had always liked her, but was too young and shy to say anything. The two eventually married in a huge ceremony attended by many of soccer's greatest players. They have three sons, Thiago, Mateo, and Ciro.

Back on the soccer pitch, during the 2008–09 season, Lionel scored thirty-eight goals in just fifty-one games as Barça won both La Liga and the Copa del Rey. Then in the Champions League final, Barça faced off against Manchester United from Great Britain and won 2–0, including a beautiful header from Lionel.

That capped a dream season, where Barça became the first Spanish club to ever win what is called a "treble," taking home all three of the most important trophies in a single year (La Liga, Copa del Rey, and Champions League).

In 2009–10, Barça again won La Liga, dropping just a single game as Lionel scored an amazing forty-seven goals in fifty-three games, to further cement his legend.

In December 2009, he was awarded the Ballon d'Or by a record margin. It was the culmination of an amazing journey—a kid from Rosario being named the best in the world at the age of twenty-two. While Lionel appreciated the honor, he was still a low-key guy and hated the fanfare. He even had to dress up, attend a banquet, and give a speech. Winning as a team and capturing all those trophies was what truly mattered to him, not an individual award.

So he took the time to thank everyone who had helped get him to this point, including his coaches and his teammates. "If I'd had a vote, I would have voted for any of the Barça players," Lionel said.

But mostly he thanked his family, "who have always been by my side."

10

The Argentine National Team

THERE ARE MANY SIMILARITIES between Lionel Messi and Diego Maradona, most notably that both are short yet possess spectacular dribbling skills, creativity, and a flair for the dramatic. Maradona scored some of the most famous goals in the history of soccer, especially during the 1986 World Cup, when, as team captain, he helped lead Argentina to victory. In terms of on-field play, Lionel was one of the few who could ever compare to him.

Off the field, they have very little in common. Lionel is quiet and private. He rarely speaks to the media or is photographed out on the town. He is content spending time with family and making sure he gets his rest. Maradona was always loud. He was a brash and cocky player with a huge personality. He said wild things to the media, got in various feuds through the years, including on-field fights, and basked in the attention. He loved the fame. He was larger than life.

Lionel is different. His reserved personality is, in part, just a product of his nature. His demeanor was also likely shaped by having moved away and needing to adapt to a new country at the young age of thirteen. Throughout his career, even as he became enormously popular in his home country, he still had to fight hard to connect with people the way Maradona effortlessly did.

Lionel knew one thing: If he could deliver a World Cup to Argentina, then there would be no doubts about his status as an Argentine soccer legend. There is simply no stage in soccer as grand as the World Cup, where national pride swells and all eyes are focused on each contest. There is added significance because the opportunities are so precious. If you lose a La Liga championship, well, there is always next year. The World Cup, however, comes just once every four years, meaning even someone with a long career might only get three or perhaps four chances to win it. Many players will get just one.

Lionel had been the star of the 2005 U-20 World Cup and for that he was rewarded with a spot on the 2006 FIFA World Cup team. The event was held in Germany and Lionel was just eighteen years old. He would score one goal, record one assist, and start a number of games, but Argentina would rely mostly on older and more established players.

In the quarterfinals, Argentina met up with power-house Germany, which, despite being located far away in Europe, was a major rival. The two countries had met in the World Cup finals in both 1986 and 1990 (and at the time, Germany was known as "West Germany"). Argentina won the first. West Germany took the second. While Argentina is known for playing with great flair and offensive push, the Germans are known to be clinical and purposeful. It is one of the great clashes of style in international soccer.

In their 2006 matchup, Argentina took a 1–0 lead. But cheered on by a rabid home crowd of 72,000 fans in Berlin, Germany tied it in the eightieth minute and then prevailed on penalty kicks, 4–2, to advance. The game was so intense that a brawl nearly broke out at one point, neither side willing to back down. Regardless, Lionel never got in the game. Argentina left one of the greatest goal scorers of all time on the bench, not even getting him in for the penalty kicks. Lionel learned how quickly a World Cup can be lost and how much Argentina despised the German team.

The World Cup loss was a disappointment, but in 2008, Lionel had the opportunity to represent Argentina at the Summer Olympics in Beijing, China.

Men's soccer at the Olympics consists of national teams featuring players under twenty-three, so at age twenty-one, Lionel qualified to play. He, like nearly everyone, found the Olympic experience magical. From the opening ceremony, to being around the best athletes in the world, to attending other events during downtime, it was a cherished moment. The USA Basketball Dream Team—including LeBron James and Kobe Bryant—was there. So too were world-class sprinter Usain Bolt and swimmer Michael Phelps.

"The fact that we have been to the athletes' village and met famous sportsmen, it's all an experience that we will not forget quickly," Lionel told the Associated Press at the time.

Argentina wasn't there to just meet people, though. They were there to win. With a deep and experienced team, they needed just two goals from Lionel to sweep through the field and defeat Nigeria for the gold medal. To have it draped around his neck and have Argentina's national anthem played remains a point of pride for Lionel. He called it his greatest sporting accomplishment.

"The Olympic gold in 2008 is the win that I value the most, because it is a tournament that you may only play in once in your lifetime," Lionel told a Spanish magazine.

By the time Lionel returned to the World Cup in 2010 in South Africa, he was the best player in the world. He was also coached by a familiar name, Diego Maradona, who had taken over the national team in an effort to return the country to glory. The two had become friendly, appreciative and respectful of each other's talents, even if they were different people. Now, though, the old legend was in charge of the young legend. And Maradona hoped Lionel would shine.

"I just wish from the bottom of my heart that Messi gets to showcase his talents and has his best performance of all time," Maradona said.

The rest of the team was lacking, however. Lionel had no one who could create opportunities for him, which left him in the role of solo playmaker. This was the opposite of how he was able to play at Barça, where he was surrounded by dangerous teammates. Unfortunately, Argentine fans expected the same level of goal scoring out of him for their team, too. When in the run-up to the World Cup, Lionel struggled to find the net, criticism mounted about his game. Lionel didn't like it and began to try to make the perfect play, rather than just rely on his natural game. That made the situation even worse.

Maradona tried to defend his star. "I don't know what people think of Leo," he said. "I can tell you what I think of him. I think he's the best in the world. And he's Argentine. I've already told the boys, 'if Leo gets the ball, we'll have plenty of chances.' . . . We need Messi to play the way he does at Barça."

Lionel understood what a great performance in the World Cup would mean for him. To this day, there remains a debate about who is better, Maradona or Messi. Maradona's talents are undeniable. At his best he was unstoppable. Yet much of his argument is based on his incredible play during the 1986 World Cup. Outside of that one month, he was never as consistently as great, especially in professional leagues, as Lionel has been. Maradona scored 356 total goals (pro and international in his career). As of 2020, Lionel is close to 700 with many more years to come before retirement.

Yet that's the power of the World Cup stage.

It's one reason why Lionel wanted to be at his very best in the tournament. Team-wise, it started well. Argentina swept through group play without losing a game. The wins were great, but Lionel didn't score a goal, suggesting that something was wrong. Lionel's scoring drought continued in a 3–1 victory over Mexico in the round of sixteen. He kept saying it wasn't a problem and that a goal would come. However, he was getting few chances and the quarterfinals brought a familiar, and stubborn, foe.

Germany.

The game was played in Cape Town, the southern-most major city in Africa. Maradona was confident that this time would be different against the mighty Germans, and in a way, he was correct. Rather than another close game, this time it wasn't even close. Germany scored on a third-minute cross and spent the rest of the day annihilating Argentina, eventually winning 4–0. It was one of the most humiliating defeats the national team had ever suffered.

"This is the most disappointing moment of my life," Maradona said after. "This is really like a kick in the face. I have no more energy for anything."

Lionel failed to score a single goal in the World Cup, despite being the reigning world player of the year. Germany exposed all of the team's problems, which is common when a flawed team suddenly faces a great opponent. Lionel was embarrassed, frustrated, and angry. He sat in a heap in the post-game locker room, mostly crying in disappointment.

"I feel really awful," Lionel was quoted as saying. "I want to go home . . . We failed to live up to every-one's expectations."

This was the first moment of utter failure in Lionel's career. Sure, he had suffered losses prior, but not many. Generally, he played, scored goals, and won. This was different. The struggles of the national team were personal, and his scoreless World Cup and early exit meant fans back home still weren't 100 percent sold on Lionel Messi as an Argentine hero. What he did for Barcelona was one thing. What he did for them was another. Now he had to wait four years to rewrite the script.

"We have to start all over again," he said.

11

World Cup

IT WAS A LONG FOUR YEARS of anticipation, but
Lionel would get another shot at the ultimate soccer
championship. The 2014 World Cup was held in
Brazil, the home of Argentina's archenemy. This
meant that Argentine fans could easily travel there to
cheer on their national team. Lionel was twenty-seven
by now, and an even better and more experienced
player. He was undoubtedly one of soccer's all-time
greats and as Argentina's captain, he was the center-
piece of the team. Maradona was no longer the
coach. A more balanced attack was in place. Lionel
felt at ease going into his best opportunity to win.

"Wearing the national shirt is something really great," Lionel said in *Messi*. "I would like to bring a lot of happiness to my people."

In the group stage opener against Bosnia and Herzegovina, Lionel had an assist and a brilliant goal where he dribbled past three defenders, causing two of them to crash into each other, before rifling a shot off the post and into the net. Argentina won, 2–1. The stands were filled with Argentines who had traveled to Brazil, making the stadium feel like this was a home game back in Buenos Aires.

"We got a fantastic reception here," Lionel said. "I wasn't expecting there to be so many Argentinians."

It was more of the same in the next game against Iran. With the score tied at 0–0, Lionel gave the fans something to cheer about. In the ninety-first minute, he innocently collected a ball about twenty-five yards out from the goal on the right side. He was well defended, but he tapped the ball toward the middle of the field and unloaded a curving shot that bent around the defender and appeared to be sailing wide before hooking back and coming just inside the far goalpost. It was his second spectacular goal in two games.

Argentina closed out group play by defeating Nigeria, 3–2, thanks to two goals from Lionel, including another bending shot that few on earth could attempt, let alone make. For Argentina, momentum was on their side heading into the knockout rounds. This was the Lionel of Barça fame, a fully engaged superstar that the Argentine fans had been desperate to see dominate in a World Cup.

"We were more threatening today, found the spaces to exploit and had more chances to score," Lionel said after the match against Nigeria. "But we still want more . . . It's a wonderful experience with the people here. We're all still chasing a shared dream."

Switzerland awaited in the round of sixteen and neither team could find the back of the net. Not through ninety minutes of regulation and not through the first fifteen minutes of extra time. As the minutes ticked away in the second period of extra time, it appeared the game would have to be decided by penalty kicks, which players dread because it's more of a skills competition than pure soccer.

Then Lionel collected a pass near midfield in the 119th minute and did what Lionel Messi does best . . . attack.

He charged forward, leaving one opponent in the dust. He dribbled through and leaped over another who attempted to slide tackle him. Now he was charging toward the box, his talent and reputation causing three Swiss defenders to converge on him and leave the other Argentine players alone.

"My first thought was to go for it myself," Lionel said. "But then I saw [teammate Angel] Di Maria appear [on the right side]."

Lionel fooled everyone by passing instead of shooting, sliding the ball over to the wide-open Di Maria, who one-timed it into the net for a thrilling, and winning, goal. Just like that, Argentina was moving on.

Di Maria got the goal, but it was Lionel who'd made the play. He was named Man of the Match despite not scoring.

"He was our water in the desert," the Argentina coach, Alejandro Sabella, said. "He, once again, gave us a chance to breathe fresh air."

But Lionel wasn't interested in basking in the victory for too long. As ever, he was focused on winning it all.

"We have to make the most of it and keep going," Lionel reminded teammates and fans.

They did, in fact, keep it going against Belgium, when Lionel helped set up an early goal and

Argentina won, 1–0. Next up, the semifinals against the Netherlands, a game in which it felt like everyone back home in Argentina was watching. By now, World Cup fever had overwhelmed the country, and fans who hadn't flown to São Paulo, Brazil, to watch in person, flocked to parties, cafes, and public squares to watch Lionel and his teammates. This is what Lionel always dreamed of delivering to his homeland, one of those incredible runs that brings a nation together.

The semifinal against the Netherlands was well played and evenly fought. Lionel almost scored early on a free kick. He almost set up a couple of teammates for goals late in the match. None got in, though. The Netherlands' defense excelled and limited his touches. They didn't want to let him beat them. Soccer is a team game, though, and Argentina's defense was also stout. Neither side scored a goal, and the game finished 0–0. The winner would be determined by penalty kicks.

This being the World Cup semifinal, it was the second-most pressurized penalty kick shootout imaginable—only the final could be bigger. Yet Lionel calmly shot his attempt, the team's first, in for a goal. It set the tone. The three Argentines who followed him all scored. Meanwhile, the Netherlands was stopped twice. Argentina advanced to the finals, courtesy of a 4–2 shootout victory.

Now the World Cup was there for the taking.

"As a player, winning a World Cup is the best there is," Lionel said. "It's something you dream about when you are a kid and it never disappears. We will do everything to make this dream a reality."

Here was the problem. Waiting in the finals was, once again, Germany, the team that had eliminated Argentina in 2006 and 2010. Lionel was the best player in the world and the best player of his generation, but Germany was a complete team, armed with stars such as Thomas Mueller and a ferocious commitment to playing a disciplined style.

This was the most important game of Lionel's career and every loose ball, every dribble, every cross and volley was fought over. The game was tight throughout. No one could score for thirty minutes, then forty-five, then an hour, then seventy and eighty and ninety minutes. It went to overtime, ten minutes, then twenty, and still it was 0–0. Back and forth the battle went, Lionel getting loose a couple of times but never quite able to score. He kept giving it his all and then finding a way to give a little bit more. Still, it wasn't enough to secure a goal. Around the world, fans were on edge, watching this incredible drama.

Finally, in the 113th minute, Germany scored. A stunned and tired Argentina tried to mount a final push to force penalty kicks, but they ran out of time. The Germans celebrated. Lionel and his teammates collapsed in exhaustion and tears.

The dream was over.

"It's very painful to lose in this manner," Lionel said. "We had the chances."

Lionel had scored four goals during the World Cup and been the most important player in carrying Argentina through the final minutes of the final contest. As a result, he was awarded the Golden Ball trophy as the tournament's best player. It was a surprising, but telling, honor. It is rare for a player on the losing team to win such an award. Even though his team didn't win, that's how great Lionel was in the World Cup.

At the time, it meant nothing to him. He was so disappointed by the loss that he couldn't even manage a smile at the trophy presentation.

"In these moments, the prize doesn't interest me at all," Lionel said. "We wanted to take home the trophy and enjoy it with all the people in Argentina. Now we carry with us the disappointment of not being able to win the match."

The World Cup loss, after getting so close, was particularly haunting for Lionel. His time with the national team contained many great moments—not just that U-20 World Cup or Olympic gold, but victories over Brazil, exciting goals, and comeback wins throughout the years. But taking a major trophy, either in World Cups or Copa Americas—a tournament contested by all the South American countries—proved elusive. Argentina lost four times in the finals of those events.

In 2016, Lionel announced he was retiring from the national team. He felt he had nothing more to give. "I tried my hardest," he said. "I want more than anyone to win a title with the national team, but unfortunately, it did not happen."

Distraught Argentine fans responded by pleading on social media for him to reconsider. They even organized a rally in a plaza in downtown Buenos Aires. Fifty thousand of them came out, held signs, and chanted, "Don't Go, Leo!"

It was enough for Lionel to unretire two years later and declare, "my love for my country and this shirt is too great." His return was great, but it didn't yield a championship. Argentina was eliminated in the round of sixteen at the 2018 World Cup. Nevertheless, it sent a powerful message to the world that despite moving to Spain at thirteen and failing to deliver a championship like Maradona, his connection with his homeland was still pure and powerful. He has said that when his Barça career ends, he might even return to Newell's Old Boys for a final season, giving him a chance to play again at home in Rosario.

Even without that World Cup, Lionel Messi was beloved in Argentina, the place that had birthed his career and a home he'd never stopped loving.

12

Hero

CAMP NOU SITS on the edge of a tightly packed neighborhood in Barcelona, towering some fifteen stories into the air. Its central location allows many Barça fans to walk to the stadium, and on game days the streets and restaurants surrounding it are alive with activity. It was built in 1957, dubbed the "new grounds" (or "Camp Nou" in Spanish), and currently seats just under a hundred thousand spectators, making it one of the largest stadiums on earth.

The seats on one side of the stadium are painted

to read *mes que un club*—"more than a club." It is a Barça motto, a phrase to highlight the connection between the team and the fans who follow it religiously, whether locally or around the globe.

It is also one of the places that Lionel Messi loves the most. And that feeling is mutual.

When full, Camp Nou is loud and vibrant, with waving flags, screaming fans, and rehearsed chants. One of the most popular is the singsong "Mess-E, Mess-E" to honor their favorite player. The people here know soccer, and they know the great fortune they've had to watch Lionel develop from a promising young graduate of La Masia into an unstoppable, championship-winning force for Barça.

"He is one step above us all," his former teammate Xavi, said. "He's the best player and there can be no argument . . . I don't ever want to compare Messi to anyone else. It just isn't fair. On them."

"I'm not sure he's human," said opponent Ander Herrera.

"Messi's like a PlayStation," said opposing coach Arsene Wenger.

The superlatives and compliments never end with Lionel. Everyone who has borne witness to him has been left in awe. The ball control. The ability to accelerate into open space. The creativity. The way he creates the smallest openings and then drills a shot through it. The improbability of his moves. The late-game heroics.

He won the Ballon d'Or, as the world's best player, in 2009, 2010, 2011, 2012, and then again in 2015. No one else had ever won the award four consecutive years, a string of genius and dominance that was almost impossible to imagine. His five awards are tied for the most ever with Cristiano Ronaldo of Portugal, and, for years, also a member of rival Real Madrid.

Lionel has also won the Golden Shoe as Europe's top goal scorer five times and was La Liga player of the year eight times and . . . the honors go on and on.

During the 2009–10 season, he scored forty-seven times in fifty-three games, almost a one-to-one ratio. In 2010–11 it was fifty-three goals in fifty-five games. Then in 2011–12 it was an astonishing seventy-three goals in sixty appearances, followed by sixty more goals in fifty games in 2012–13.

El Clásico games, at least two per season, between Barça and Real Madrid, featuring Cristiano Ronaldo, became not just major events within La Liga, but moments when fans around the world would stop and pay attention. The 2014 game, where Lionel netted a hat trick to deliver a 4–3 victory, drew an estimated global television audience of 400 million, more than the NFL Super Bowl.

Lionel and Cristiano were clearly the two best players in the world and two of the best of all time. During the ten-year stretch from 2008–2017, they each won the Ballon d'Or five times and in most of the years the other was the runner-up. Sometimes the votes were extremely close. The fact that they played each other so often was a treat. When Ronaldo left Madrid in 2018 to play for Juventus in Italy's Serie A league, Lionel admitted he missed the regular battles. So too did the fans, media, and fellow players who constantly debated which of the two superstars was better.

In truth, they were both great and they had different styles on the field and different personalities off it. Cristiano was known to be fiery and outspoken, and, of course, Lionel was quieter. As such, they were not close friends and rarely interacted away from the game. They did, however, motivate each other to elevate their play higher and higher. It was like a game of anything-you-can-do-I-can-do-better. They admitted to keeping an eye on each other, watching highlights of beautiful runs or amazing goals and then trying to one-up the other.

"I think we push each other sometimes in the competition, this is why the competition is so high," Cristiano told CNN.

Lionel agreed, "I have learned a lot from him over the years."

As for the debate over who was the better player, that was mostly left to everyone else. "Some people say I'm better, other people say it's him," Cristiano told CNN, although he thought the argument didn't make sense since they had different styles. "You can't compare a Ferrari with a Porsche because it's a different engine . . . He does the best things for Barcelona. I do the best things for Madrid."

Barça won the majority of the head-to-head clashes between the two, further endearing Lionel to the fans. And after many of the goals Lionel scored, he would point to the sky to honor his grandmother Celia, who had first pushed him to play. She passed away when he was ten and never saw him reach the biggest stages of soccer.

"I dedicate my goals to my grandmother," Lionel said. "She took me to football but now she can't see how far I have come. Nevertheless, she continues to help me and my family."

Other times he also kisses the Barcelona crest on his jersey. As someone who started with the club at such a young age, his love for Barça is nearly lifelong, the way it is for many fans. To Lionel, both post-goal gestures represent family. His real one and his Barça one.

In 2012, while playing for both Barça and Argentina, Lionel scored a world-record ninety-one goals in just sixty-nine appearances. That's 1.32 goals a game. It shattered the record previously held by Gerd Muller, who scored eighty-five for Bayern Munich and Germany way back in 1972. While there is an old saying that "records are made to be broken," breaking this one will require an historic season by someone truly incredible in the future.

Yet all these awards and records are individual accomplishments, whereas Lionel is all about team championships because soccer is a team sport. Across his career, he has led Barça to nine La Liga titles, six Copa del Reys, seven Supercopa de Españas (another Spanish tournament), four Champions League trophies, and three FIFA Club World Cups, in which Barça played the best pro teams across the globe.

One of his proudest accomplishments came during the 2014–15 season, when he teamed up with Luis Suárez of Uruguay and Neymar of Brazil, to form an all–South American attack for Barça. Dubbed by fans "MSN" (each of their initials), the trio scored 122 combined goals, the most ever in a season for a Spanish professional team.

In doing so, Barça won La Liga and Copa del Rey. It then capped the "treble" by taking the Champions League title. By repeating their 2008–09 feat (which just seven European teams have ever accomplished), Barça became the first to do it twice. Their status as soccer kings was unquestioned.

That, of course, is how Lionel always approaches the game. He isn't playing for second place.

"The objective is the same every season, try to win everything," Lionel said.

With each goal, each YouTube highlight, each trophy, each honor, and each jersey sold, Lionel became a bigger and bigger star. He is one of the most famous people on the planet, recognizable on every continent.

His contracts with Barcelona soared above $40 million per year. Combined with his endorsement deals and revenue sharing from merchandise, *Forbes* estimated he made $154 million in 2018 alone. He has starred in advertisements, television shows, and movies. His YouTube videos, including advertisements, have annually ranked among the most watched on the media platform. Children and pets have been named after him.

He was one of the first people on earth to amass over 100 million followers on Instagram and he did it with fewer posts than anyone else. Lionel needed just 354 posts, while others who have achieved it, such as Selena Gomez, Kim Kardashian, and Cristiano Ronaldo, had 1,000 or more posts.

That, though, speaks to the true Lionel— immensely popular yet stubbornly private. Even as fans desperately seek any bit of information about him, he offers few interviews with the media and attempts to shield his private life as much as possible. He is most content spending time with his wife and children, not to mention extended family and old friends.

While fabulously wealthy, he isn't known to flash his possessions or even spend very much. For security and privacy, he and his family do live in a large house outside Barcelona surrounded by a high wall. The property features both a pool and its own small soccer field, for training or just playing with the kids.

"We're not people who waste money on luxury items," Lionel said in *Messi*. Instead, he is more likely to dedicate himself to charity. He's worked for years with the United Nations Children's Fund (UNICEF) and raised money for Doctors Without Borders and for victims of natural disasters from Haiti to Japan. The Lionel Messi Foundation doles out additional money around the globe and often stages games to raise funds.

Back in Argentina, he has personally funded numerous soccer organizations, helping build education and training facilities for Newell's Old Boys and even its rival, Rosario Central, not to mention clubs in Buenos Aires. He's paid the salaries of staffers at the Argentine Football Association during difficult times. He's been particularly committed to improving training and soccer pitches in his old neighborhood in Rosario.

He is, he promises, mostly the same kid who grew up there. The money and fame and accomplishments haven't changed him. He may be the greatest player on earth, but he is still the Flea who found joy in the game playing on humble South American streets.

"It's true," he said in *Messi*. "I live the same life as always. The only thing is, that if I want to go out with my family in Rosario, I can't [due to crowds of fans seeking selfies and autographs]."

Other than that, he is still Leo.

"I have my feet firmly on the ground and I never forget where I came from."

Just give him a ball and watch him go.

Instant Replay

JUST SHORT OF MIDFIELD, LIONEL RECEIVES A PASS.

LIONEL DRIBBLES PAST ONE DEFENDER AS ANOTHER CHASES AFTER HIM.

WITH DEFENDERS IN PURSUIT, LIONEL BLAZES TOWARD THE GOAL.

LIONEL DRIBBLES AROUND A SLIDING DEFENDER.

GETAFE'S GOALIE DIVES FOR THE BALL AND MISSES!

Lionel scores one of the most amazing goals in soccer history.

The Nonstop Sports Action Continues!

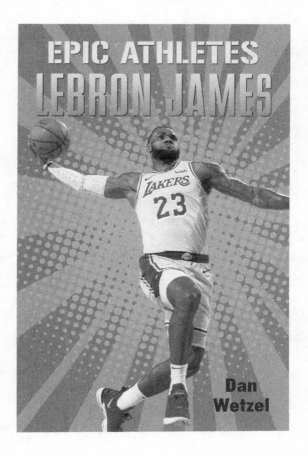

EPIC ATHLETES

LEBRON JAMES

LAKERS
23

Dan
Wetzel

1

The Block

EACH AND EVERY FAN, nearly twenty thousand in total, was on their feet inside Oracle Arena in Oakland, California. Standing in front of their seats. Standing on their seats. Standing in the aisles. They were too nervous to sit, after all.

With two minutes left in Game 7 of the 2016 NBA Finals, the Cleveland Cavaliers and the Golden State Warriors were tied 89–89. In addition to the twenty thousand in attendance, there were 44.5 million people tuned in to their televisions watching across America, and many millions more around the world.

While all those people were watching, LeBron James was searching—searching for a way to impact the game and seize a championship because he suddenly couldn't hit a jump shot. During the biggest moment of the biggest series, a series in which he'd averaged almost thirty points a game, LeBron couldn't make a basket.

In the final five minutes of the game, he missed from twenty-two feet, he missed from thirteen feet, he missed from two feet. He wasn't alone. The pressure was impacting everyone; the best players in the world were struggling with the intensity of the moment. LeBron's teammate Kyrie Irving had clanked a shot. So had fellow Cavalier Kevin Love. For the Warriors, Steph Curry had missed; so had Klay Thompson, Draymond Green, and Andre Iguodala.

Cleveland and Golden State had been battling for more than two and a half hours on this Father's Day. They had been going back and forth over nearly two weeks of this epic June championship clash. The action had been so even that not only was The Finals tied at three games apiece, and not only was this decisive game tied at 89, but at that very moment, each team had scored 699 cumulative points in the series. Everything was deadlocked.

Something had to give, though. There could only be one champion.

For LeBron, losing wasn't an option. He'd come too far to get to this point, to have this opportunity. He knew it meant too much to everyone not just back in Cleveland, but in all of Ohio, including the city of Akron, where he had grown up with a single mother and been a highly publicized star athlete since he was a kid.

He'd started his career with the Cavaliers in 2003 as the number one overall draft pick directly out of high school. He'd been crowned a basketball king before he ever stepped on a National Basketball Association (NBA) court and, by the age of eighteen, he'd already drawn comparisons to the legendary Michael Jordan, considered by many the greatest player of all time. But after seven seasons, even as he developed into the best player in the NBA, he couldn't win a championship. So, he left for Miami as a free agent.

Doing so angered fans back home in Ohio. They burned his jersey and cursed his name. They felt betrayed as he won two titles with the Miami Heat. Those should have been Cleveland's championships, they thought. Those should have been their victory parades, they complained.

Hungry for More EPIC ATHLETES? Look Out for These Superstar Biographies, in Stores Now!

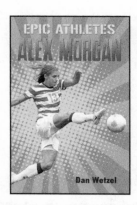

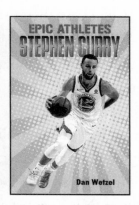

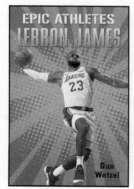

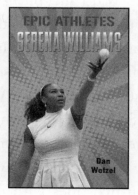

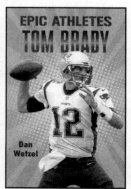